NEGROES WITH GUNS

Robert Williams in 1967.

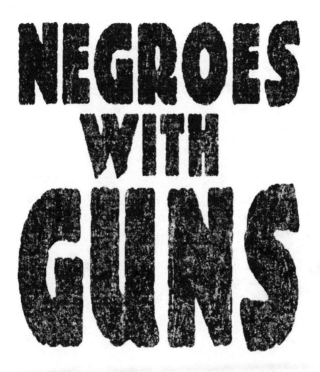

NEGROES WITH GUNS

Robert F. Williams
Foreword by Gloria House
Introduction by Timothy B. Tyson

Wayne State University Press   Detroit

African American Life Series

*A complete listing of the books in this series
can be found online at http://wsupress.wayne.edu.*

Series Editors

Melba Joyce Boyd
Department of Africana Studies, Wayne State University

Ronald Brown
Department of Political Science, Wayne State University

Originally published in 1962 by Marzani & Munsell, Inc.,New York.
Reprinted 1998 by Wayne State University Press.
Foreword copyright © 1998 by Gloria House.
Introduction copyright © 1998 by Timothy B. Tyson
ISBN-13: 978-0-8143-2714-2 ISBN-10: 0-8143-2714-1

15 14 13 12 11   13 12 11 10 9

Library of Congress Cataloging-in-Publication Data

Williams, Robert Franklin, 1925–
    Negroes with guns / Robert F. Williams ; introduction
by Timothy B. Tyson ; foreword by Gloria House.
        p. cm.—(African American Life)
    Originally published: New York : Marzani & Munsell,
[c1962]. With new introd. and foreword.
    ISBN 0-8143-2714-1 (pbk. : alk. paper)
    1. Afro-Americans—Civil rights—North Carolina—
Monroe—History—20th century.   2. Monroe (N.C.)—
Race relations.   3. Violence—North Carolina—
Monroe—History—20th century.   4. Self-defense—
North Carolina—Monroe—History—20th century.
5. Williams, Robert Franklin, 1925– . I. Title.
II. Series.
F264.M75W5   1998
975.6′755—dc21   98-10737

Designer: Mary Primeau

Contents

Foreword

Gloria House

In August 1965, Ruby Sales, Joyce Stokes, and I sat on filthy bunks in the Lowndes County Jail in Hayneville, Alabama, singing freedom songs with the brothers who had been locked in cells on the second floor. We could hear them well, and raised our voices as loudly as possible—to be heard by them, and to distract ourselves from our dismal surroundings. The jail floor was awash with spillovers from poorly working toilets; we kept our feet up on the lice-ridden mattresses, and tried not to be overwhelmed by the stench. We were waiting for Scott B. Smith and Stokely Carmichael (now Kwame Ture), themselves only recently released from the jail, and the Student Non-Violent Coordinating Committee (SNCC) staff in Selma to try to raise our bail. As we tried to keep ourselves occupied, we overheard a newscast on a deputy's radio that a riot was occurring in Watts, California. We identified with that community instantly, feeling that those brothers and sisters, in venting their resentment against oppressive conditions, somehow acted as our very own champions as we sat behind bars.

After almost two weeks in the Hayneville jail, we were forced out at gun point. Minutes later, when we had walked only a block away, a member of our group, Jonathan Daniels, an Episcopal seminarian, was murdered as we watched in horror. Father Richard Morrisroe, a Catholic priest from Chicago, was wounded in the back so critically that he required years of rehabilitative therapy before he could walk again. Both men had come to the South to take part in the civil rights movement. Lowndes County officials had planned to kill Jonathan and Fr. Morrisroe to frighten and dissuade other whites from involvement in the movement.

Our group had picketed a store in Hayneville for about half an hour before the sheriff ordered us arrested, hauled onto a garbage truck, and dumped at the county jail. Two weeks later, after the local officials had sufficient time to identify and deputize a marksman, the guards came to our cells and told us that we were being released on our own recognizance. We hadn't received word from the SNCC office in Selma concerning such an arrangement, so didn't believe what we were being told. We refused to leave the jail, suspecting there might be foul play. The guards then forced us at gunpoint to leave the jail and its surrounding property. As we turned onto the main street and approached a nearby store, we heard gunfire. Not knowing at the time that the two white demonstrators were targeted, we were terrified that all of us would die on that curiously deserted main street in the county seat. When the shooting stopped, we ran from house to house, trying to arouse help for Fr. Morrisroe, who was moaning in excruciating pain. No one opened to us; they had been notified that there would be killings. In their retreat behind closed doors, "ordinary" citizens collaborated in the murder and crippling of young men who had come seeking justice.

Experience of subtle and blatant abuse of our human rights was typical in the daily life of freedom workers. Combat zones like the Hayneville main street characterized the South during the period. Racist citizens and "law officers" could abuse, intimidate, abduct, and murder civil rights workers with full support and protection of the legal system. Jonathan Daniels' killer was acquitted, as were many others who killed in the cause of race supremacy.

Before finally finding the bodies of Andrew Goodman, James Chaney and Michael Schwerner in a dam, Mississippi law officers unearthed many Black bodies from the rivers of Mississippi. The abduction and murder of two white youngsters, Goodman and Schwerner, and the appeal of their families to the national government, had prompted a search that would not have been carried out had all three freedom workers been African Americans. No such searches had been conducted to ensure that Black families could give proper burials to loved ones who had been "disappeared" in the course of struggle. Most Americans associate official kidnapping, torture, and murder of human rights activists with the practices of South American dictators. They would resist seeing the activities of their own officials in this light.

The menace of unmitigated violence inundated the Southern air like a heavy, suffocating humidity. Everyone on the side of justice had to push against this weight; but those outside the movement did not perceive it, understand it, or give it serious consideration as a crucial factor impacting every Black person's daily existence. Outside the movement, people seemed oblivious to whites' derisive sneers whenever they came in contact with freedom workers, unaware of the jailings, the nighttime drive-by shootings, the evictions, the setting afire of homes and churches, the beatings in isolated, secret places; the instances in which demonstrators were spat upon, the harassment with vicious dogs and other forms of terror and abuse to which Blacks in the South were routinely subjected. The United States government arrogantly condemns other countries for such human rights violations.

Today, more than thirty years since the so-called civil rights period, historians continue to disregard the staggering burden these forms of violence imposed upon Black communities. Perhaps we will never know the total number of casualties in this domestic war on African Americans, and we have still to answer the question: When people are subjected to unrelenting violence by organized citizens and their government collaborators, what recourse do they have? Robert Williams's *Negroes with Guns* requires us to reassess this issue.

Negroes with Guns chronicles Williams's involvement in the civil rights movement of Monroe, North Carolina. Recounting several cases in which the human rights of individuals and the Black community at large were violated, Williams shows how the community's policy of self-defense developed, and why the local activists came to support his conclusion that they had to "meet violence with violence."

In 1955 Williams returned to Monroe from service in the U.S. Marines. Wanting to help make life better in his community, he assumed leadership of the local NAACP chapter. The legal cases that he relates emerged from civil rights struggles advanced by the community. The grievances involved, which were never redressed by the legal system, reflect some of the most brutal forms of dehumanization—a Black woman hotel worker kicked down a flight of stairs by a white customer, two young boys jailed for expressing affection to a playmate, attempted rape of a pregnant Black woman, organized vigilante attacks on Black neighborhoods and freedom workers.

Since the Justice Department, the Federal Bureau of Investigation, and local law enforcers refused to provide protection while surreptitiously supporting and enabling the perpetrators of violence, the Monroe Black community had no alternative but to arm itself and fight back. The Williams home became a focus of hatred and armed attacks as the Monroe movement continued. However, when Black men organized armed defense teams and returned fire, the racist mobs lost their nerve. Confirming the cowardice inherent in mob mentality, Williams concluded that racists who might ruthlessly destroy a community if they alone have weapons will cease fighting when they discover that Blacks are armed, for they find it "impossible to stomach the thought of violence" if *their lives* are at risk.

Three decades after the first publication of *Negroes with Guns*, there is still much to learn from Williams's experience and philosophy. First, it is important to be clear that Williams advocated self-defense, not aggression. He reminded the nation that when African American militants protect their people, they are not *introducing* violence, they are combatting it. He pointed out that "when people say that they are opposed to Negroes 'resorting to violence,' what they really mean is that they are opposed to Negroes defending themselves and challenging the exclusive monopoly of violence practiced by white racists."

Second, Williams did not suggest that armed self-defense was the whole answer. He maintained that self-defense should function as a critical component in a broadly conceived strategy for liberation, along with other non-violent forms of struggle. He advised that a community's self-defense readiness could secure a safer environment in which non-violent campaigns would have greater chance of success. This theory merits further consideration by contemporary activists, for given the persistence of the Ku Klux Klan and the rise of right-wing militia and other neo-Nazi organizations in the United States, we cannot predict what attacks individuals and communities of color may face in coming years. In March 1996, a "skinhead" soldier in the U.S. Army was convicted for arbitrarily murdering a Black couple to prove himself a loyal Nazi.

The nation turned a petrified gaze on Monroe's self-defense actions; government and establishment representatives lost no time condemning Williams and pressuring African Americans to do likewise. The NAACP appears to have been all too willing to comply, withdrawing financial support from the Monroe chapter when it was desperately needed, undermining Williams's leadership, vilifying him in the national press, and finally suspending him from office as local president. That the NAACP national leadership acted on behalf of the so-called liberal power structure to police Williams and the Monroe community holds another lesson. Williams was one of the first African American leaders with courage enough to say publicly, "there must be a struggle within our own ranks to take leadership away from the black Quislings who betray us."

Many African Americans and our leaders are in deep denial concerning the tragic status of the majority of our population. It is still easy for some to pretend that racism, discrimination, and control of government by private corporations are not causative factors in widescale poverty, unemployment, disease, homelessness, stupendous incarceration rates for young Black males, the flow of drugs and automatic weapons into *our* communities, and fratricide among our youth. To advance their own political careers, some Black leaders form alliances with those whose policies sabotage community-building efforts by African Americans. With only recent access to halls of power in cities where we are the majority, African Americans are reluctant to denounce the leaders who sell them out. We don't want to split ranks, to air dirty laundry for national television, even when matters of justice and human rights are at stake. What social advances are we sacrificing through such duplicity? Williams's book inspires us to find a stronger collective backbone.

Negroes with Guns raises yet another unresolved issue: the devaluation and degradation of African American women by the larger society. A few cases cited by Williams concerned the Monroe community's attempt to protect Black women from racist, sexist attacks. These cases illustrate sharply the dehumanizing ways in which African American women have been viewed and treated historically. Racist white men in Monroe and throughout the South took for granted that they could disrespect Black women, exploit them and assault them at will, impelled by anger or lust. Though contemporary activists and scholars have focused a good deal of their energy on eradicating the negative images associated with Black women, and healing the wounds of historic abuse, we have not yet been able to get rid of the stereotypes which provide Euro-American society a rationalization for its denigration of African American women.

In terms of a legacy of struggle, perhaps Williams's most significant contribution was his effort to situate the African American liberation struggle in the context of the entire world. He rejected labels that would frame the movement in too narrow terms. He was a humanist and an internationalist, someone who identified with all the world's oppressed. He enlightened them about us, and us about them. He was our liaison, pulling us onto the world stage, and out of the confines of the "civil rights" struggle. Williams knew that the African American movement of the 1960s was part of the post–World War II movement of people of color worldwide, who fought off foreign rule and all forces that constrained their freedom. In developing solidarity with the peoples of Cuba, Vietnam, China, and other Third World countries, Williams offered a model for a twenty-first–century internationalism.

A man of immense personal courage and vision, Williams foresaw before the cycle of urban rebellions that began with Watts that there would be "many more racial explosions in the days to come. Monroe was just the beginning." His prediction must be reflected upon, for racism continues to fracture American society, violence still pervades every aspect of our lives, and government "law enforcement" policies steadily erode our human rights. One may be certain that the question of self-defense will emerge again for national discussion.

Introduction: Robert F. Williams, "Black Power," and the Roots of the African American Freedom Struggle

■ ■

Timothy B. Tyson

Negroes with Guns is one of the most telling and important documents of the African American freedom struggle.
Hammered together by exile Robert F. Williams and editor
Marc Schlieffer in Havana in 1962, this book influenced a generation of young black insurgents and helped to lay the
groundwork for the Black Power movement. *Negroes with
Guns* fascinated Huey P. Newton and became the most important intellectual influence on the Black Panther Party for
Self-Defense in Oakland, California.[1] Historians August Meier
and Elliott Rudwick observe that Williams "had a profound
effect" within the Congress of Racial Equality.[2] Williams also
had a significant influence among members of the Student
Nonviolent Coordinating Committee in the South and among
residents of inner-city ghettos across the country.[3] A play
based on *Negroes with Guns,* Frank Greenwood's "If We Must
Live," ran in community theaters in the Watts section of Los
Angeles for six months in 1965 to standing ovations from
eager crowds.[4] For members of the Revolutionary Action
Movement, the Republic of New Africa, and for many other
young race rebels, *Negroes with Guns* became a kind of bible
of black militance. It was not that Williams advocated violence against white people, Anne Braden, of the Southern
Conference Educational Fund, noted in a review published
in 1963.[5] Williams "merely articulated what many people feel

and what many more people will express unless change comes rapidly."

African Americans, however, were not waiting on the federal government to rescue them. "Armed self-defense is a fact of life in black communities—north and south," one North Carolina activist wrote to Williams in 1965, "despite the pronouncements of the 'leadership.' "[6] By the end of the decade, of course, many of the views that Williams expressed in the late 1950s would seem commonplace. But *Negroes with Guns* does more than introduce us to a prophetic figure, a harbinger of the violent upheavals to come. It captures for us a snapshot of the movement at what Martin Luther King, Jr. called "a stage of profound crisis."[7] When *Negroes with Guns* appeared in 1962, the Montgomery Bus Boycott was six years in the distance and nonviolence had produced little in the way of tangible political results. The country's response to the United States Supreme Court's 1954 mandate to desegregate "with all deliberate speed" demonstrated no speed and little deliberation. As *Negroes with Guns* went to press, legal victories had produced only a wave of white terrorism, a smattering of token concessions, and a host of elaborate evasions of the law; nonviolent direct action had little to show for all the brutality it had unleashed in its opponents. On the side streets and back roads of the "civil rights"–era South, whatever dramas might play out in the public square by day, black activists slept lightly and kept their guns close at hand. *Negroes with Guns* gives us a remarkably vivid and accurate glimpse of the brutal and authentic political terrain that activists of the African American freedom movement sought to transform. It also affords us the best available view of a remarkable mind of the South, Robert F. Williams, one of the most dynamic race rebels of a generation that changed the world.

Robert Williams was born in 1925 to Emma C. and John L. Williams. His father was a railroad boiler washer in Monroe, North Carolina, a town of six thousand in the North Carolina piedmont.[8] Women born in slavery still tended vegetable gardens along the street where young "Rob" Williams grew up. His grandfather, Sikes Williams, born a slave in Union County, had attended Biddle Institute in nearby Charlotte after Emancipation and became one of Union County's first black schoolteachers.[9] He enlisted as a Republican activist during the late 1800s and "traveled all over the county and the State making speeches and soliciting support for the Party."[10] Sikes Williams also published a small newspaper called "The People's Voice."[11] The interracial "fusion" coalition of Republicans and Populists which he had labored to build won every statewide office in 1896. "THE CHAINS OF SERVITUDE ARE BROKEN," Williams and his interracial allies proclaimed to their black constituents that year. "NOW NEVER LICK THE HAND THAT LASHED YOU."[12] Two years later, however, white conservatives overthrew the democratic process. In a campaign of fraud and violence all across the state in 1898, the party of white supremacy seized what Democratic editor Josephus Daniels celebrated as "permanent good government by the party of the white man."[13]

Robert's grandmother, Ellen Isabel Williams, lived through all of these struggles and was "my greatest friend," he wrote later.[14] "She read *everything*," he recalled, and "specialized in history." Ellen Williams would point to the iron printing press rusting in the shed and tell the young boy stories of Sikes Williams and the crusading editor's political exploits. She reminded her grandson that she had been conceived in the union of her mother with their master, Daniel Tomblin. Before she died, Ellen Williams handed young Robert a gift that symbolized much that slavery and the struggle for liberty had taught her: she gave him the ancient rifle that his grandfather had wielded against white terrorists at the turn of the century.[15]

In 1946, 21-year-old Robert Williams stepped down from a segregated Greyhound in the uniform of his country. Military training had given black veterans "some feeling of security and self-assurance," he recalled. "But most of all they taught us to use arms."[16] Like thousands of other black veterans, Robert Williams did not come home to pick cotton.[17]

Another returning black veteran, a friend of Williams's named Bennie Montgomery, did come home to raise cotton on the farm that his father operated as a sharecropper for

W. W. Mangum, a large-scale white landowner near Monroe. Saturday, June 1, 1946, was a regular workday on the Mangum place, but Montgomery asked Mangum for his wages at noon, explaining that he needed to go to Monroe and have his father's car repaired. Mangum apparently kicked and slapped the young veteran, and Montgomery pulled out a pocketknife and cut his employer's throat. The Ku Klux Klan wanted to lynch the black sharecropper, but instead the state police whisked Montgomery out of town, tried and convicted him of murder, and ten months later executed him in the gas chamber at Central Prison in Raleigh.[18]

State authorities shipped the sharecropper's remains back to Monroe. Robbed of their lynching, however, the local chapter of "the invisible empire" let it be known that Bennie Montgomery's body belonged not to his family, but to the Ku Klux Klan. "They was gonna come and take Bennie's body out and drag it up and down the streets," J. W. McDow, another African American veteran, recalled. "I rather die and go to hell before I see that happen."[19] A group of former soldiers met at Booker T. Perry's barbershop and made a battle plan. When the Klan motorcade pulled up in front of Harris Funeral Home, 40 black men leveled their rifles, taking aim at the line of cars. Not a shot was fired; the Klansmen simply weighed their chances and drove away. Former U.S. Army PFC Robert F. Williams carried a carbine that night. So did three of the men who would become key lieutenants in the "black militia" that Williams organized ten years later.[20] "That was one of the first incidents," Williams recalled, "that really started us to understanding that we had to resist, and that resistance could be effective if we resisted in groups, and if we resisted with guns."[21]

Williams was in the Marine Corps in 1954 when he heard that the United States Supreme Court had struck down school segregation. "At last I felt that I was a part of America and that I belonged," he wrote.[22] "I was sure that this was the beginning of a new era of American democracy."[23] When he came back to Monroe, however, he discovered that the *Brown* decision and the 1956 triumph of the Montgomery Bus Boycott provoked Ku Klux Klan rallies near

Monroe with crowds as big as 15,000.[24] "The echo of shots and dynamite blasts," the *Southern Patriot* reported in 1957, "has been almost continuous throughout the South."[25] The Monroe NAACP dwindled to six members who then contemplated disbanding. When the newest member objected to dissolution, the departing membership chose him to lead the chapter. "They elected me president," Robert Williams recalled, "and then they all left."[26] Finding himself virtually a one-man NAACP chapter, Williams turned first to the black veterans with whom he had stood against the Klan that night back in 1946. Another veteran, Dr. Albert E. Perry, became vice president. Recruiting from the beauty parlors, pool halls, and street corners, Williams built a cadre of almost two hundred members within a year.[27] The Monroe branch of the NAACP became "the only one of its kind in existence," Julian Mayfield wrote in *Commentary* in 1961. "Its members and supporters, who are mostly workers and displaced farmers, constitute a well-armed and disciplined fighting unit."[28]

Under the leadership of Williams and Perry, the Monroe NAACP soon launched a campaign in 1957 to desegregate the local tax-supported Monroe Country Club, where white children enjoyed free swimming lessons while black children swam in farm ponds and drainage ditches. Harry Golden, a prominent Jewish liberal from nearby Charlotte, called the Monroe swimming pool crusade "unwise and unrealistic." Golden thought it "naive" of Williams to "experiment with the crude emotions of a small Southern agricultural community."[29] But the decision to target the swimming pool was not a matter of ideology or tactics; several local African American children had drowned in these isolated and unsafe "swimming holes." Golden was right, however, about what "crude emotions" could incite. The Ku Klux Klan blamed Dr. Perry for the resurgent black activism and a large, heavily-armed Klan motorcade attacked the physician's home one night that summer. Black veterans greeted the nightriders with sandbag fortifications and a hail of disciplined gunfire. The Monroe Board of Aldermen immediately passed an ordinance banning Ku Klux Klan motorcades, a measure they had refused to consider prior to the gun battle.[30]

An even more vivid local drama dragged Monroe onto the stage of international politics on October 28, 1958. Two African American boys, "Fuzzy" Simpson and Hanover Thompson, ages eight and ten, met some white children in a vacant lot. A kissing game ensued in which the ten-year-old Thompson and an eight-year-old white girl named Sissy Sutton kissed one another.[31] Rarely in history does an incident so small open a window so large into the life of a place and a people, a window that revealed both the visceral power of sexual questions in racial matters and the complex dynamics of Cold War politics for the African American freedom struggle.[32]

After the kissing incident, Sissy Sutton's mother reported that she "would have killed Hanover myself if I had the chance."[33] The girl's father took a shotgun and went looking for the two boys. Neighbors reported that a white mob had roared up to the Thompson home and threatened not only to kill the boys but to lynch their mothers.[34] Later that afternoon, police officers spotted Hanover Thompson and Fuzzy Simpson pulling a wagon loaded with soft drink bottles. "Both cops jumped out with their guns drawn," Thompson recalled. "They snatched us up and handcuffed us and threw us in the car. When we got to the jail, they drug us out of the car and started beating us." The local juvenile court judge reported to Governor Hodges that the police had detained the boys "for their own good, due to local feeling in the case."[35]

Authorities held the two boys for six days without permitting them to see parents, friends, or attorneys. Passing gunmen fired dozens of shots into the Thompson home. Klan terrorists torched crosses on the lawn.[36] For many white citizens, the case seemed to confirm the sexual fears that accompanied their vision of where school desegregation would lead. "If [black children] get into our rural schools and ride the buses with our white children," one local woman wrote, "the Monroe 'kissing' incident is only a start of what we will have."[37] On November 4, Judge J. Hampton Price convened what he termed "separate but equal" hearings for the white parents and the black boys.[38] Denied the right to engage counsel or to confront their accusers, Hanover Thompson and Fuzzy Simpson were sentenced to Morrison Training School For Negroes. If they behaved well, Judge Price told the boys, it might be that they could be released *before* they were twenty-one.[39]

Robert Williams saw in the "Kissing Case" not only the irritational sexual lynch-pin of white supremacy but a unique political opportunity. The Monroe NAACP set in motion what *Time* magazine called "a rolling snowball" of worldwide publicity.[40] In front of audiences across the country, Williams told stories of the two incarcerated boys and the freedom struggle in the South. Soon the "Kissing Case" emblazoned front pages around the globe, forcing Governor Hodges to hire a team of professors from the University of North Carolina at Chapel Hill to translate the tens of thousands of letters that poured into his office.[41] John Shure, head of the United States Information Agency at the Hague, reported that he himself had received over 12,000 letters "even though the response does not appear to have been organized."[42] While the White House and the State Department expressed alarm at the damage to U.S. foreign relations, Williams had a ready answer: "If the U.S. government is so concerned about its image abroad, then let it create a society that will stand up under world scrutiny."[43]

Governor Hodges soon launched a public relations campaign of his own to, as an aide urged the governor, "give the NAACP a taste of its own medicine . . . [and] place the whole Confederacy in your debt." The aide suggested to the governor that "by hitting directly at the communist connection, we might be able to convince people of the insincerity of these protests."[44] The Federal Bureau of Investigation wrote to Governor Hodges that "Robert Williams has been under investigation for a considerable period of time" and that "you would have access to this information if you desire."[45] The governor's office then announced that the entire affair had been "a Communist-directed front," that the families of both boys were "shiftless and irresponsible," and that Hanover Thompson's mother had "a reputation for using her daughters in prostitution."[46] The USIA and the U.S.

State Department broadcast these charges around the world, apparently without convincing anyone. Three and a half months after Hanover and Sissy had kissed each other, Governor Hodges announced under enormous political pressure that "the home conditions have improved to the extent that the boys can be given conditional release."[47]

The dynamics of racial conflict in Monroe not only undercut U.S. foreign policy but undermined the strategy of the national NAACP. The "Kissing Case" gained Robert Williams national attention. What was not well known was that some of the friends and allies he made during this period—including Malcolm X, who invited him to speak at Harlem's Temple Number 7—raised money to buy military weapons for the Monroe NAACP.[48] The national office could not come to grips with either the urgent realities of racial politics in Monroe or the insurgent style of Robert F. Williams. The NAACP generally shunned so-called "sex cases" and any alliances that might leave the organization open to red-baiting.[49] Should the NAACP "ever get identified with communism," Kelly Alexander, head of the North Carolina Conference of Branches, told a reporter, "the Ku Klux Klan and the White Councils will pick up the charge that we are 'reds' and use it as a club to beat us to death."[50] Differences over strategy became bitter; Alexander complained to the national office that Williams "has completely turned his back on the one organization that is responsible for him being in the spotlight today," while Williams griped that Alexander "sounds more like a *Tom* than ever."[51] Roy Wilkins, the executive secretary of the national organization, began to refer to Williams in private as "Lancelot of Monroe."[52]

In the late spring of 1959, two news stories from other parts of the South gripped black America. One was the lynching of Mack Charles Parker, accused of raping a white woman in Mississippi. Parker had been dragged from his cell and murdered by a mob that happened to have the jailer's keys.[53] When Mississippi NAACP field secretary Medgar Evers heard the news of the Parker lynching, he told his wife, "I'd like to get a gun and start shooting."[54] The other was the terrifying ordeal of four young black college students at

Florida A&M. Their double date after the college dance was interrupted by four white men with guns and knives. The drunken assailants forced the two 18-year-old black men to kneel at gunpoint while they undressed the two women and decided aloud which one they would kidnap and then gang-rape.[55] In the wake of these notorious outrages, NAACP executive secretary Roy Wilkins conceded in a letter marked "NOT FOR PUBLICATION" that "I know the thought of violence has been much in the minds of Negroes."[56] By early May, Wilkins admitted, the NAACP found it "harder and harder to keep feelings from boiling over in some of our branches."[57]

Right on the heels of the Parker lynching and the terrors in Tallahassee, two pressing local matters brought Robert Williams and a crowd of black women to the Union County courthouse. B. F. Shaw, a white railroad engineer, was charged with attacking an African American maid at the Hotel Monroe. Georgia White, her attacker explained to the magistrate, had disturbed his sleep. Stepping into the hallway in his underwear, Shaw had struck the woman with his fist and kicked her down a flight of stairs. Slated for trial the same day, Lewis Medlin, a white mechanic, was accused of having beaten and sexually assaulted Mary Ruth Reid, a pregnant black woman, in the presence of her five children.[58] According to Williams, the black women of the Monroe NAACP had urged that two new machine guns that Julian Mayfield had smuggled into Monroe be tried out on Medlin before his trial.[59] "I told them that this matter would be handled through the law and the NAACP would help," Williams recalled, "that we would be as bad as the white people if we resorted to violence."[60]

The proceedings against the two white men compelled Williams to reconsider. The judge dropped the charges against Shaw in spite of the fact that he failed even to appear for court.[61] During the brief trial of Medlin, his attorney argued that he had been "drunk and having a little fun" at the time of the assault. Further, Medlin was married, his lawyer told the jury, "to a lovely white woman . . . the pure flower of life . . . do you think he would have left this pure flower for *that?*" He gestured toward Mary Ruth Reid, who began to cry uncontrollably.[62] Lewis Medlin was acquitted in minutes. Robert Williams recalled that "the [black] women in the courtroom made such an outcry, the judge had to send Medlin out the rear door." The women then turned on Williams and bitterly shamed him for failing to see to their protection.[63]

At this burning moment of anger and humiliation, Robert Williams turned to wire service reporters and declared that it was time to "meet violence with violence." Black citizens unable to enlist legal support must defend themselves. "Since the federal government will not stop lynching, and since the so-called courts lynch our people legally," Williams declared, "if it's necessary to stop lynching with lynching, then we must resort to that method."[64] The next day Williams revised his remarks and specifically disavowed the reference to lynching. "I do not mean that Negroes should go out and attempt to get revenge for mistreatments or injustice," he added, "but it is clear that there is no . . . court protection of Negroes' rights here, and Negroes have to defend themselves on the spot when they are attacked by whites."[65]

Banner headlines flagged these words as symbols of "a new militancy among young Negroes of the South."[66] Enemies of the NAACP blamed this "bloodthirsty remark" squarely on the national office. "Hatred is the stock in trade of the NAACP," Thomas Waring of the Charleston *News and Courier* charged. "High officials of the organization may speak in cultivated accents and dress like Wall Street lawyers, but they are engaged in a revolutionary enterprise."[67] That very morning, when he read the words "meet violence with violence" on the UPI wire, Roy Wilkins telephoned Robert Williams to inform him that he had been removed from his post as president of the Monroe NAACP.[68]

The 50th anniversary convention of the NAACP that summer of 1959 became a highly public show trial whose central issue was whether or not Robert Williams would remain suspended. The national office printed up a pamphlet, "The Single Issue In The Robert Williams Case," and distributed it to all delegates.[69] "The national office not only controlled the platform," Louis Lomax wrote, but "they subjected the Williams forces to a heavy bombardment from the NAACP's big guns." Thurgood Marshall visited the New York offices of the FBI on June 4, 1959 and urged agents to investigate Williams "in connection with [Marshall's] efforts to combat communist attempts to infiltrate the NAACP," an FBI memorandum stated.[70] Roy Wilkins twisted every available arm. Martin Luther King deployed his eloquence. Daisy Bates, the heroine of Little Rock, agreed to denounce Williams for advocating armed self-defense after the national office consented to buy $700 a month in "advertising" from her newspaper so that she could pay armed guards at her home.[71] Forty speakers, including King, Bates, and dozens of distinguished lawyers, rose one after the other to denounce Williams. But when the burly ex-Marine from Monroe finally strode down the aisle to speak, he was neither intimidated nor penitent.[72]

"There is no Fourteenth Amendment in this social jungle called Dixie," Williams declared. "There is no equal protection under the law." He had been angry, they all knew, trials had beset him, but never had he intended to advocate acts of war. Surely no one believed that. But if the black men of Poplarville, Mississippi had banded together to guard the jail the night that Mack Parker was lynched, he said, that would not have hurt the cause of justice. If the young black men who escorted the co-ed who was raped in Tallahassee had been able to defend her, Williams reminded them, such action would have been legal and justified "even if it meant that they themselves or the white rapists were killed." "Please," he beseeched the assembly, "I ask you not to come crawling to these whites on your hands and knees and make me a sacrificial lamb." And there the pleading stopped. "We as men should stand up as men and protect our women and children," Williams declared. "I am a man and I will walk upright as a man should. I WILL NOT CRAWL."[73] In a controversy that the *Carolina Times* called "the biggest civil rights story of the year," however, the NAACP convention upheld the suspension of Robert Williams.[74] The next day, Daisy Bates wrote to the Attorney General of the United States to complain about dynamite attacks on her home in Little Rock: "We have been compelled to employ private guards," she wrote.[75]

Two weeks after the 1959 NAACP convention, FBI agents reported to J. Edgar Hoover that Williams "had recently begun selling a newsletter known as *The Crusader* on the streets of Monroe."[76] *The Crusader*'s self-proclaimed mission was "ADVANCING THE CAUSE OF RACE PRIDE AND FREEDOM." Sample mailings yielded several thousand subscribers across the country for *The Crusader*. Within weeks, the first published biography of Martin Luther King, Jr. appeared, hastily-assembled by a member of the Southern Christian Leadership Conference's board of directors. It was called *Crusader Without Violence*.[77]

These developments reflected the fact that, as Anne Braden of the Southern Conference Educational Fund wrote in late 1959, "the great debate in the integration movement in recent months has been the question of violence vs. non-violence as instruments of change."[78] In a series of public debates, Williams faced King, A. J. Muste, Bayard Rustin, David Dellinger, and others. He "drew a large audience to his debate with the pacifists," George Weissman of the Socialist Workers Party wrote to Carl Braden in Louisville, "and handled himself quite well."[79] Among white Southerners, Williams argued, "there is open defiance to law and order throughout the South today." Where law and order have broken down, he said, only self-defense can prevent murder by armed zealots who either believe they are killing for God or have abandoned conscience altogether. Always careful to endorse the methods espoused by King, Williams made the case for flexibility: "nonviolence is a very potent weapon when the opponent is civilized, but nonviolence is no repellent for a sadist." Furthermore, he pointed out, "nowhere in the annals of history does the record show a people delivered from bondage by patience alone."[80]

In a response to Williams published in *Liberation* and widely reprinted, Martin Luther King, Jr. conceded that white violence had brought the movement to "a stage of profound crisis." The Supreme Court's 1954 mandate and even the triumph at Montgomery had yielded small tokens, elaborate evasions, and widespread terror. Only three responses presented themselves. One could practice "pure nonviolence," King said, but this path "could not readily attract large masses, for it requires extraordinary discipline and courage." A position that encompassed legitimate self-defense was more practical. King pointed out that "all societies, from the most primitive to the most cultured and civilized, accept [self-defense] as moral and legal. The principle of self-defense, even involving weapons and bloodshed, has never been condemned, even by Gandhi." Here was where King the politician sensed his constituency. "When the Negro uses force in self-defense," King continued, "he does not forfeit support—he may even win it, by the courage and self-respect it reflects." This widely accepted position was, of course, precisely Williams's view—which was King's problem.

The third and most unacceptable position, King argued, was "the advocacy of violence as a tool of advancement, organized as in warfare, deliberately and consciously." Here, then, was the pale beyond which King sought to cast his adversary. "Mr. Robert Williams would have us believe that there is no collective or practical alternative," King insisted. "He argues that we must be cringing and submissive or take up arms." Essentially, Dr. King had invented his own Williams, a kind of black Geronimo plotting military strikes against the white man, and then responded to *that* Robert Williams instead of the calm but defiant man who had spoken. Lacking theological training and combative in his manner, Williams was vulnerable to this caricature. But the philosophical position from which King centered his own argument—preferring nonviolence, but endorsing "the principle of self-defense, even involving weapons and bloodshed"—was precisely the position that Williams had taken.[81]

In 1961, Reverend Paul Brooks, employed by King's Southern Christian Leadership Conference, and James Forman, soon to become president of the Student Nonviolent Coordinating Committee, came to Monroe in the company of 17 Freedom Riders fresh out of jail in Jackson, Mississippi. The young insurgents arrived in Monroe to launch a nonviolent campaign in Robert Williams's backyard, though Forman later denied any intention to undermine Williams. One of the Freedom Riders announced that he had come to Monroe because he considered "Mr. Robert F. Williams to be the most dangerous person in America." Another proclaimed: "If the fight for civil rights is to remain nonviolent, we must be successful in Monroe. What happens here will determine the course taken in many other communities throughout the South."[82]

Williams had a similar understanding of the stakes. "I saw it first as a challenge," he recalled, "but I also saw it as an opportunity to show that what King and them were preaching was bullshit."[83] Two weeks of picketing at the Union County Courthouse grew progressively more perilous for the Freedom Riders. Crowds of hostile white onlookers grew larger and larger. Finally, on Sunday afternoon, August 28, a mob of more than 5,000 furious white people attacked the 30 demonstrators, badly injuring many. The nonviolent crusade swiftly deteriorated into mob gun battles. After a long night of terror, Williams and his family fled first to Canada, then on to Cuba, to escape the hordes of FBI agents who combed the countryside in search of them. One of the agents assigned to search for Williams reported his frustrations to FBI Director J. Edgar Hoover: "Subject has become something of a 'John Brown' to Negroes around Monroe and they will do anything for him."[84]

The FBI dragnet never snared Williams, but it did not take Hoover long to hear from him. Every Friday night from 11:00 to midnight on Radio Havana, Williams hosted "Radio Free Dixie," a program that from 1961 to 1964 could be heard as far away as New York and Los Angeles. Taped copies of the program circulated in Watts and Harlem.[85] From Cuba, Williams continued to edit *The Crusader* for about 40,000 subscribers.[86] Copies of *The Crusader* traveled down the Mississippi backroads with Student Nonviolent Coordinating Committee organizers; in 1964, when SNCC began to veer away from nonviolence, members cited Williams approvingly in the fierce internal debates.[87]

Though he became friends with Che Guevara and Castro himself, Williams yearned to return home and resisted the pressure to make his own politics conform to the Soviet line. Williams persuaded Castro to let him travel to North Vietnam in 1964, where he swapped Harlem stories with Ho Chi Minh and wrote propaganda aimed at African American soldiers.[88] In 1965, the Williams family relocated to Beijing, where they became friends with Mao Tse Tung and moved in the highest circles of the Chinese government for three years. When the Nixon administration moved toward opening diplomatic relations with China in the late 1960s, Williams bartered his almost exclusive knowledge of the Chinese government for safe passage home and a Ford Foundation-sponsored post at the Center For Chinese Studies at the University of Michigan.[89] Robert Williams spent the last 27 years of his life as a writer and activist in the small, trout-fishing village of Baldwin, Michigan. At his funeral in Monroe, North Carolina on November 22, 1996, Mrs. Rosa Parks told the congregation that she and those who marched with Martin Luther King, Jr. in Alabama had always admired Robert Williams "for his courage and his commitment to freedom. The work that he did should go down in history and never be forgotten."[90] Above the desk where Williams completed his memoirs just before his death, there still hangs an ancient rifle—a gift, he said, from his grandmother.

Notes

1. In late September of 1966, Hugh Pearson reports, Huey P. Newton and Bobby Seale sat in the library of the North Oakland Center and constructed the theoretical basis for the Black Panther Party for Self-Defense, relying heavily on *Negroes with Guns*. See Hugh Pearson, *The Shadow of the Panther: Huey Newton and the Price of Black Power in America* (Reading, Mass: Addison-Wesley, 1994), 28, 109. David Horowitz, who worked closely with the Black Panthers for a time, calls *Negroes with Guns* the most important intellectual influence on Newton. See Peter Collier and David Horowitz, *Destructive Generation: Second Thoughts about the Sixties* (New York: Summit,

1989), 146. Clayborne Carson names Williams as one of two central influences—the other being Malcolm X—on the formation of the Black Panthers. See Clayborne Carson, "The Black Panther Party," in *Encyclopedia of the American Left,* ed. Mari Jo Buhle et al. (Urbana: University of Illinois Press, 1992), 96.

2. August Meier and Elliott Rudwick, *CORE: A Study in the Civil Rights Movement, 1942–1968* (Urbana: University of Illinois Press, 1975), 202–4.

3. Danny Lyons, *Memories of the Civil Rights Movement* (Chapel Hill: University of North Carolina Press, 1992), 147.

4. Anne Leslie, "Exciting in Form, Ugly in Content," (Los Angeles) *People's World,* July 3, 1965, p. 3. "LIVE is only running out of bookings now," Frank Greenwood wrote to Williams six months after the play opened. "We appeared in Watts and really shook up and inspired the brothers out there. . . . My folks are ready, man! And particularly the young ones. . . . We did a free show for Watts and Venice teenagers at the center and afterwards they got up en masse and applauded." See Frank Greenwood to Robert F. Williams, December 1, 1965, box 1, Robert F Williams Papers, Bentley Historical Library, University of Michigan, Ann Arbor, hereafter cited as Williams Papers.

5. Anne Braden, *Southern Patriot* 21, no. 2 (February 1963): 2.

6. Clyde Appleton to Robert F. Williams, September 20, 1965, box 1, Williams Papers.

7. Martin Luther King, Jr., "The Social Organization of Nonviolence," in *A Testament of Hope: The Essentials Writings and Speeches of Martin Luther King, Jr.,* ed. James M. Washington (San Francisco: HarperCollins, 1991), 31.

8. Marcellus Barksdale, "Robert F. Williams and the Indigenous Civil Rights Movement in Monroe, North Carolina," *Journal of Negro History* 69, no. 2 (spring 1984): 75; H. Nelson Walden, *History of Monroe and Union County* (Monroe, 1963), 15.

9. S. E. Williams, "Application Blank No. 15," John Herman Williams Collection. I am grateful to Mr. Williams for sharing this and other family documents.

10. *Crusader* 1, no. 4 (July 18, 1959): 2; "The History of Our Family Reunion," Robert and Mabel Williams Family Collection. I am grateful to Mrs. Mabel R. Williams for sharing family documents.

11. Robert F. Williams interview transcript, Robert C. Cohen Papers, State Historical Society of Wisconsin, hereafter cited as Cohen Papers, 53; *Monroe Enquirer-Journal,* "Monroe Historical Edition," September 1974, 4-B.

12. "To the Colored Voters of Union County," campaign flyer from Black History file, The Heritage Room, Union County Courthouse, Monroe, North Carolina.

13. See J. Morgan Kousser, *The Shaping of Southern Politics: Suffrage Restriction and the Establishment of the One-Party South* (New Haven: Yale University Press, 1974), 76.

14. Robert Williams, "Someday I'm Going Back South," *Daily Worker*, Detroit edition, April 9, 1949.
15. *Crusader* 1, no. 4 (July 18, 1959): 2; "The History Of Our Family Reunion," Robert and Mabel Williams Family Collection; Tyson interview with Robert F. Williams, September 2, 1996.
16. Transcript of the Robert F. Williams interview with James Mosby, 18, Ralph Bunche Oral History Collection, Moorland-Spingarn Research Center, Howard University, hereafter cited as Williams interview with Mosby.
17. John Dittmer, *Local People: The Struggle For Civil Rights In Mississippi* (Urbana: University of Illinois Press, 1994), 1–9.
18. *Monroe Enquirer*, June 31, 1946, 1, and March 31, 1947, 1.
19. J. W. McDow interview with Timothy B. Tyson, September 17, 1993, hereafter cited as McDow interview.
20. McDow interview; Woodrow Wilson interview with Marcellus Chandler Barksdale, Duke Oral History Collection, hereafter cited as Wilson interview with Barksdale; B. J. Winfield interview with Marcellus Chandler Barksdale, Duke Oral History Collection, hereafter cited as Winfield interview with Barksdale.
21. Williams interview with Mosby.
22. *Southern Patriot* 18, no. 11 (January 1960): 3.
23. Clayborne Carson et al., eds., *The Eyes on the Prize Reader* (New York: Penguin, 1991), 36.
24. (Charleston) *News and Courier*, September 21, 1956, 1-B, reports attendance at a Union, South Carolina rally at 12,000 to 15,000. *Monroe Enquirer*, March 17, 1958, 1, estimates that "last year . . . cross-burnings and meetings here attracted thousands."
25. *Southern Patriot* 15, no. 1 (January 1957): 1.
26. Williams interview with Mosby.
27. Williams, *Negroes with Guns* (New York: Marzani & Munsell, Inc., 1962), 50–51; McDow interview; Winfield interview with Barksdale; Wilson interview with Barksdale; Williams interview with the author; Williams interview with Mosby.
28. Julian Mayfield, "Challenge to Negro Leadership: The Case of Robert Williams," *Commentary*, April 1961, 298.
29. Harry Golden, "Monroe, North Carolina and the 'Kissing Case,' " *Carolina Israelite*, January 1955, 9 and January–February, 1959, 2.
30. "Article III Parades, Cavalcades, and Caravans," in *Code of The City of Monroe*, 473–475, North Carolina Collection, University of North Carolina at Chapel Hill.
31. Kelly Alexander to Roy Wilkins, "A Report of Activities of the North Carolina State Conference of Branches in Reference to the Case of David Simpson and James H. Thompson of Monroe, North Carolina," December 26, 1958, NAACP Papers.
32. See Patrick Jones, " 'Communist Front Shouts Kissing Case to the World:' The Committee to Combat Racial Injustice and the Politics of Race and Gender During the Cold War," M.A. thesis, University of Wisconsin, 1996.

33. George Weissman, "The Kissing Case," *Nation*, January 17, 1959, 47.

34. Gloster B. Current to Roy Wilkins, December 23, 1958, NAACP Papers. See also *Charlotte Observer*, January 12, 1959, 2-A; *Carolina Times*, January 10, 1959, 1; *Monroe Enquirer*, November 20, 1958, 1.

35. James Hanover Thompson interview with Timothy B. Tyson, May 13, 1993, hereafter cited as Thompson interview; J. Hampton Price to Luther H. Hodges, November 26, 1958, Box 423, "Segregation" folder, Governor Luther H. Hodges Papers, North Carolina Department of Archives and History, hereafter cited as Hodges Papers.

36. Thompson interview; *Chicago Defender*, January 17, 1959, 3.

37. *Charlotte Observer*, February 2, 1959, 2-B.

38. Chester Davis, "Press in North Gives Distorted Versions," (Winston-Salem) *Journal and Sentinel*, February 8, 1958, 1.

39. "Transcript of Statements Made by Attorney Conrad Lynn During Interview on the 'Frank Ford Show,' Radio Station WPEN, Philadelphia, Pennsylvania on June 20, 1959, from 12:40 until 1:35 AM," NAACP Papers.

40. The *Time* story, which appeared in the international edition of the magazine, was reprinted in full in the *Monroe Enquirer*, February 9, 1959, 1.

41. Robert E. Giles to University of North Carolina President William C. Friday, February 6, 1959, Hodges Papers.

42. Basil L. Whitener to Luther H. Hodges, March 2, 1959, Hodges Papers.

43. Williams recounted these remarks in *Crusader* 4, no. 2 (August 1962): 4.

44. John Briggs to Bill Sharpe, cc to Luther H. Hodges, February 23, 1959; Bill Sharpe to Luther H. Hodges, February 12, 1959; Luther H. Hodges to Bill Sharpe, February 19, 1959, all in Hodges Papers.

45. O. L. Richardson to Luther H. Hodges, n.d., Hodges Papers.

46. Chester Davis, "Communist Front Shouts Kissing Case to the World," (Winston-Salem) *Journal and Sentinel,* February 8, 1958, 1.

47. *Monroe Enquirer*, February 16, 1959, 1.

48. Cohen Papers, 382. Malcolm referred to Williams as "my very good friend." See David Gallen, ed., *Malcolm X as They Knew Him* (New York: Carrols' Graf, 1992), 164.

49. Dan T. Carter, *Scottsboro: A Tragedy of the American South* (Baton Rouge: Louisiana State University Press, 1969).

50. Chester Davis, "Communist Front Shouts Kissing Case to the World," 1.

51. Kelly M. Alexander to Roy Wilkins, "A Report of Activities of the N.C. Conference of Branches in Reference to the Case of David Simpson and James Thompson of Monroe, N.C.," NAACP Papers; Robert F. Williams to George Weissman, December 17, 1958, Committee to Combat Racial Injustice Papers, State Historical Society of Wisconsin, University of Wisconsin, hereafter cited as CCRI Papers.

52. Roy Wilkins to P. L. Prattis, "Personal, Not For Publication," May 28, 1959, NAACP Papers.

53. Howard Smead, *Blood Justice: The Lynching of Mack Charles Parker* (New York: Oxford University Press, 1986).

54. Mrs. Medgar Evers with William Peters, *For Us, the Living* (New York: Ace, 1970), 194.

55. Roy Wilkins, "Report of the Secretary to the Board of Directors for the Month of April 1959," NAACP Papers. See also *Washington Post*, May 3, 1959, 4; (Baltimore) *Afro-American*, May 9, 1959; (Durham) *Carolina Times*, May 23, 1959, 1; *New York Times*, May 7, 1959, 22.

56. Roy Wilkins to P. L. Prattis, "Personal, Not for Publication," May 28, 1959, NAACP Papers.

57. *Afro-American*, May 30, 1959, 4; Roy Wilkins, *Standing Fast: The Autobiography of Roy Wilkins* (New York: Penguin, 1982), 265.

58. *Monroe Enquirer*, January 26, 1959, 1, and March 9, 1959, 1; *New York Post*, January 27, 1959, 4, May 7, 1959, 1, November 11, 1959, 1; *Crusader* 4, no. 7 (April 1963): 4; *Carolina Times*, February 7, 1959, 2, and January 31, 1959, 1.

59. Julian Mayfield, in his unpublished autobiography, claims that "a famous black writer made touch with gangsters in New Jersey and bought me two sub-machine guns which I took to Monroe." See Julian Mayfield, "Tale From The Lido," Julian Mayfield Papers, The Schomberg Center for the Study of Black Culture, New York Public Library. I am grateful to Kevin Gaines for sharing these materials.

60. Williams interview with Mosby.

61. Referral From May 11 Board Meeting," 1; *Southern Patriot*, vol. 18, no. 11 (January 1960): 3.

62. *New York Post*, May 7, 1959; *Monroe Enquirer*, May 7, 1959, 1; see also Jones, " 'Communist Front Shouts Kissing Case to the World,' " 127.

63. Williams interview with Mosby.

64. "Rec'd via phone from UPI—May 6, 1959," NAACP Papers; *New York Times*, May 7, 1959, 22.

65. "Roy Wilkins, Executive Secretary, Complainant, against Robert F. Williams, Respondent, Brief for Respondent," 1–2, NAACP Papers.

66. *New York Times*, May 7, 1959, 22; (Jackson, Mississippi) *State-Times*, 1.

67. *News and Courier*, May 7, 1959.

68. Text of telegram from Roy Wilkins to Robert Williams, May 6, 1959, NAACP Papers.

69. "The Single Issue in the Robert Williams Case," CCRI Papers.

70. Federal Bureau of Investigation Subject File, Thurgood Marshall, telegram from SAC, New York to Director, FBI, June 5, 1959. My thanks to Alex Charns for sharing these documents.

71. Daisy Bates to Roy Wilkins, July 23, 1959, Daisy Bates Papers, State Historical Society of Wisconsin.

72. Louis Lomax, *The Negro Revolt* (New York: Signet, 1962), 112–114.

73. *Pittsburgh Courier*, July 25, 1959, 1; *Crusader*, July 25, 1959, 1.

74. *Carolina Times*, January 5, 1960, 1.

75. Daisy Bates, *The Long Shadow of Little Rock* (New York: David McKay Co., 1962), 162.

76. Robert Franklin Williams Federal Bureau of Investigation subject file, in possession of the author, hereafter cited as RFW/FBI.

77. L. D. Reddick, *The Crusader without Violence: A Biography of Martin Luther King, Jr.* (New York: Harper and Brothers, 1959).

78. *Southern Patriot* 18, no. 11 (January 1960): 3.

79. George Weissman to Carl Braden, October 20, 1959, Carl and Anne Braden Papers, State Historical Society of Wisconsin. See also *Crusader* 1, no. 14 (September 26, 1959): 6.

80. *Liberation*, September 1959. See also Carson et al., *Eyes on the Prize Reader*, 110–13.

81. Carson et al., *Eyes on the Prize Reader*, 110–113.

82. *Crusader* 3, no. 6 (August 21, 1961): 3; James Forman interview with Timothy B. Tyson, January 17, 1997.

83. Williams interview with Mosby.

84. RFW/FBI.

85. Robert Perkins to Robert F. Williams, Robert F. Williams Papers, University of Michigan.

86. United States Senate, Ninety-first Congress, Second Session, Part 1, Hearings Before the Subcommittee to Investigate the Administration of the Internal Security Act and Other Internal Security Laws of the Committee on the Judiciary, Testimony of Robert F. Williams, February 16, 1970, 90.

87. Danny Lyons, *Memories of the Southern Civil Rights Movement* (Chapel Hill: University of North Carolina Press, 1992), 147.

88. Sidney Rittenberg, "Recollections of Robert Williams," May 4, 1997, unpublished essay in possession of the author. See also Cohen Papers, 312; "Listen, Brother," Williams Papers.

89. Rittenberg, "Recollection of Robert Williams," 3. See also Williams, "While God Lay Sleeping: The Autobiography of Robert F. Williams," typescript in the possession of Timothy B. Tyson, 237–319. My thanks to Robert Williams and the Williams family for sharing this manuscript.

90. Mrs. Rosa Parks, eulogy for Robert Williams, November 22, 1996, Central Methodist Church, Monroe, North Carolina.

NEGROES
WITH
GUNS

WANTED BY THE FBI

INTERSTATE FLIGHT – KIDNAPING
ROBERT FRANKLIN WILLIAMS

Photograph taken May, 1961

FBI No. 84,275 B

Aliases: Bob Williams, Robert F. Williams.

DESCRIPTION

Age:	36, born February 26, 1925, Monroe, North Carolina		
Height:	6'	**Complexion:**	dark brown
Weight:	240 pounds	**Race:**	Negro
Build:	heavy	**Nationality:**	American
Hair:	black	**Occupations:**	free lance writer, freight
Eyes:	brown		handler, janitor, machinist

Scars and Marks: scar left eyelid, scar left nostril, scar on calf of right leg.

Fingerprint Classification: 19 L 1 R 100 8 Ref: T R T
M 1 T 10   A A T

CAUTION

WILLIAMS ALLEGEDLY HAS POSSESSED A LARGE QUANTITY OF FIREARMS, INCLUDING A .45 CALIBER PISTOL WHICH HE CARRIES IN HIS CAR. HE HAS PREVIOUSLY BEEN DIAGNOSED AS SCHIZOPHRENIC AND HAS ADVOCATED AND THREATENED VIOLENCE. WILLIAMS SHOULD BE CONSIDERED ARMED AND EXTREMELY DANGEROUS.

A Federal warrant was issued on August 28, 1961, at Charlotte, North Carolina, charging Williams with unlawful interstate flight to avoid prosecution for kidnaping (Title 18, U. S. Code, Section 1073).

IF YOU HAVE INFORMATION CONCERNING THIS PERSON, PLEASE NOTIFY ME OR CONTACT YOUR LOCAL FBI OFFICE. TELEPHONE NUMBER IS LISTED BELOW.

DIRECTOR
FEDERAL BUREAU OF INVESTIGATION
UNITED STATES DEPARTMENT OF JUSTICE
WASHINGTON 25, D. C.
TELEPHONE, NATIONAL 8-7117

Wanted Flyer No. 290
September 6, 1961

Prologue

■ ■

Why do I speak to you from exile?

Because a Negro community in the South took up guns in self-defense against racist violence—and used them. I am held responsible for this action, that for the first time in history American Negroes have armed themselves as a group to defend their homes, their wives, their children, in a situation where law and order had broken down, where the authorities could not, or rather would not, enforce their duty to protect Americans from a lawless mob. I accept this responsibility and am proud of it. I have asserted the right of Negroes to meet the violence of the Ku Klux Klan by armed self-defense—and have acted on it. It has always been an accepted right of Americans, as the history of our Western states proves, that where the law is unable, or unwilling, to enforce order, the citizens can, and must, act in self-defense against lawless violence. I believe this right holds for black Americans as well as whites.

Many people will remember that in the summer of 1957 the Ku Klux Klan made an armed raid on an Indian community in the South and were met with determined rifle fire from the Indians acting in self-defense. The nation approved of the action and there were widespread expressions of pleasure at the defeat of the Kluxers who showed their courage by running away despite their armed superiority. What the nation doesn't know, because it has never been told, is that the Negro community in Monroe, North Carolina, had set the example two weeks before when we shot up an armed motorcade of the Ku Klux Klan, including two police cars, which had come to attack the home of Dr. Albert E. Perry, vice-president of the Monroe chapter of the National Associ-

3

ation for the Advancement of Colored People. The stand taken by our chapter resulted in the official re-affirmation by the NAACP of the right of self-defense. The Preamble to the resolution of the 50th Convention of the NAACP, New York City, July 1959, states: ". . . we do not deny, but reaffirm, the right of an individual and collective self-defense against unlawful assaults."

Because there has been much distortion of my position, I wish to make it clear that I do not advocate violence for its own sake or for the sake of reprisals against whites. Nor am I against the passive resistance advocated by the Reverend Martin Luther King and others. My only difference with Dr. King is that I believe in flexibility in the freedom struggle. This means that I believe in non-violent tactics where feasible; the mere fact that I have a Sit-In case pending before the U.S. Supreme Court bears this out. Massive civil disobedience is a powerful weapon under civilized conditions where the law safeguards the citizens' right of peaceful demonstrations. In civilized society the law serves as a deterrent against lawless forces that would destroy the democratic process. But where there is a breakdown of the law, the individual citizen has a right to protect his person, his family, his home and his property. To me this is so simple and proper that it is self-evident.

When an oppressed people show a willingness to defend themselves, the enemy, who is a moral weakling and coward, is more willing to grant concessions and work for a respectable compromise. Psychologically, moreover, racists consider themselves superior beings and are not willing to exchange their superior lives for our inferior ones. They are most vicious and violent when they can practice violence with impunity. This we have shown in Monroe. Moreover, when because of our self-defense there is a danger that the blood of whites may be spilled, the local authorities in the South suddenly enforce law and order when previously they had been complacent toward lawless, racist violence. This too we have proven in Monroe. It is remarkable how easily and quickly state and local police control and disperse lawless mobs when the Negro is ready to defend himself with arms.

Furthermore, because of the international situation, the Federal Government does not want racial incidents which draw the attention of the world to the situation in the South. Negro self-defense draws such attention, and the Federal Government will be more willing to enforce law and order if the local authorities don't. When our people become fighters, our leaders will be able to sit at the conference table as equals, not dependent on the whim and the generosity of the oppressors. It will be to the best interests of both sides to negotiate just, honorable and lasting settlements.

The majority of white people in the United States have literally no idea of the violence with which Negroes in the South are treated daily—nay, hourly. This violence is deliberate, conscious, condoned by the authorities. It has gone on for centuries and is going on today, every day, unceasing and unremitting. It is our way of life. Negro existence in the South has been one long travail, steeped in terror and blood—our blood. The incidents which took place in Monroe, which I witnessed and which I suffered, will give some idea of the conditions in the South, conditions that can no longer be borne. That is why, one hundred years after the Civil War began, we Negroes in Monroe armed ourselves in self-defense and used our weapons. We showed that our policy worked. The lawful authorities of Monroe and North Carolina acted to enforce order *only after, and as a direct result of, our being armed.* Previously they had connived with the Ku Klux Klan in the racist violence against our people. Self-defense prevented bloodshed and forced the law to establish order. This is the meaning of Monroe and I believe it marks a historic change in the life of my people. This is the story of that change.

Chapter 1

Self-Defense Prevents Bloodshed

In June of 1961 the NAACP Chapter of Monroe, North Carolina, decided to picket the town's swimming pool. This pool, built by WPA money, was forbidden to Negroes although we formed one quarter of the population of the town. In 1957 we had asked not for integration but for the use of the pool one day a week. This was denied and for four years we were put off with vague suggestions that someday another pool would be built. Two small Negro children had meantime drowned swimming in creeks. Now, in 1961, the City of Monroe announced it had surplus funds, but there was no indication of a pool, no indication of even an intention to have a pool. So we decided to start a picket line. We started the picket line and the picket line closed the pool. When the pool closed the racists decided to handle the matter in traditional Southern style. They turned to violence, unlawful violence.

We had been picketing for two days when we started taking lunch breaks in a picnic area reserved for "White People Only." Across from the picnic area, on the other side of a stream of water, a group of white people started firing rifles and we could hear the bullets strike the trees over our heads. The chief of police was on duty at the pool and I appealed to him to stop the firing into the picnic area. The chief of police said, "Oh, I don't hear anything. I don't hear

Segregation

anything at all.'' They continued shooting all that day. The following day these people drifted toward the picket line firing their pistols and we kept appealing to the chief of police to stop them from shooting near us. He would always say, "Well, I don't hear anything."

The pool remained closed but we continued the line and crowds of many hundreds would come to watch us and shout insults at the pickets. The possibility of violence was increasing to such a proportion that we had sent a telegram to the U.S. Justice Department asking them to protect our right to picket. The Justice Department referred us to the local FBI. We called the local FBI in Charlotte and they said this was not a matter for the U.S. Justice Department; it was a local matter and they had checked with our local chief of police, who had assured them that he would give us ample protection. This was the same chief of police who had stood idly by while these people were firing pistols and rifles over our heads, the same chief of police who in 1957 had placed two police cars in a Klan motorcade that raided the Negro community.

Attempt to Kill Me

On Friday, June 23, 1961, I went into town to make another telephone call to the Justice Department. While I was there I picked up one of the pickets and started back to the line at the swimming pool, which was on the outskirts of town. I was driving down U.S. Highway 74 going east when a heavy car (I was driving a small English car, a Hillman), a 1955 DeSoto sedan, came up from behind and tried to force my lighter car off the embankment and over a cliff with a 75-foot drop. I outmaneuvered him by speeding up and getting in front of him. Then he rammed my car from the rear and locked the bumper and started a zig-zag motion across the highway in an attempt to flip my light car over. The bumpers were stuck and I didn't use the brake because I didn't want to neutralize the front wheels.

We had to pass right by a highway patrol station. The

station was in a 35-mile-an-hour zone and by the time we passed it the other car was pushing me at 70 miles an hour. I started blowing my horn incessantly, hoping to attract the attention of the highway patrolmen. There were three patrolmen standing on the opposite side of the embankment in the yard of the station. They looked at the man who was pushing and zig-zagging me across the highway and then threw up their hands, laughed, and turned their backs to the highway.

He kept pushing me for a quarter of a mile until we came to a highway intersection carrying heavy traffic. The man was hoping to run me out into the traffic, but about 75 feet away from the highway I was finally able to rock loose from his bumper, and I made a sharp turn into the ditch.

My car was damaged. The brake drum, the wheels, and the bearings had been damaged, and all of the trunk compartment in the rear had been banged in. After we got it out of the ditch, I took the car back to the swimming pool and showed it to the chief of police. He stood up and looked at the car and laughed. He said, "I don't see anything. I don't see anything at all." I said, "You were standing here when I left." He said, "Well, I still don't see anything." So I told him I wanted a warrant for the man, whom I had recognized. He was Bynum Griffin, the Pontiac-Cheverolet dealer in Monroe. He said, "I can't give you a warrant because I can't see anything that he's done." But a newspaperman standing there started to examine my car, and when the chief of police discovered that a newspaperman was interested, then he said, "Well, come to the police station and I'll give you a warrant."

When I went to the police station he said, "Well, you just got a name and a license number and I can't indict a man on that. You can take it up with the Court Solicitor." I went to the Court Solicitor, which is equivalent to the District Attorney, and he said, "Well, all you got here is a name and a number on a piece of paper. I can't indict a man on these grounds." I told him that I recognized the man and mentioned his name. He said, "Wait a minute," and he made a telephone call. He said, "I called him and he said he didn't do that." I again told him that I had recognized the man and that I had the license number of the car that he had used.

8

Finally the Court Solicitor said, "Well, if you insist, I'll tell you what you do. You go to his house and take a look at him and if you recognize him, you bring him up here and I'll make out a warrant for him." I told him that was what the police were being paid for, that they were supposed to go and pick up criminals. So they refused to give me a warrant for this man at all.

What happens when the Police are criminals?

"God Damn, The Niggers Have Got Guns!"

The picket line continued. On Sunday, on our way to the swimming pool, we had to pass through the same intersection (U.S. 74 and U.S. 601). There were about two or three thousand people lined along the highway. Two or three policemen were standing at the intersection directing traffic and there were two policemen who had been following us from my home. An old stock car without windows was parked by a restaurant at the intersection. As soon as we drew near, this car started backing out as fast as possible. The driver hoped to hit us in the side and flip us over. But I turned my wheel sharply and the junk car struck the front of my car and both cars went into a ditch.

Then the crowd started screaming. They said that a nigger had hit a white man. They were referring to me. They were screaming, "Kill the niggers! Kill the niggers! Pour gasoline on the niggers! Burn the niggers!"

We were still sitting in the car. The man who was driving the stock car got out of the car with a baseball bat and started walking toward us saying, "Nigger, what did you hit me for?" I didn't say anything to him. We just sat there looking at him. He came up close to our car, within arm's length with the baseball bat, but I still hadn't said anything and we didn't move in the car. What they didn't know was that we were armed. Under North Carolina state law it is legal to carry firearms in your automobile so long as these firearms are not concealed.

I had two pistols and a rifle in the car. When this fellow started to draw back his baseball bat, I put an Army .45 up in the window of the car and pointed it right into his face and didn't say a word. He looked at the pistol and he didn't say anything. He started backing away from the car.

Somebody in the crowd fired a pistol and the people again started to scream hysterically, "Kill the niggers! Kill the niggers! Pour gasoline on the niggers!" The mob started to throw stones on top of my car. So I opened the door of the car and I put one foot on the ground and stood up in the door holding an Italian carbine.

All this time three policemen had been standing about fifty feet away from us while we kept waiting in the car for them to come and rescue us. Then when they saw that we were armed and the mob couldn't take us, two of the policemen started running. One ran straight to me, grabbed me on the shoulder, and said, "Surrender your weapon! Surrender your weapon!" I struck him in the face and knocked him back away from the car and put my carbine in his face, and I told him we were not going to surrender to a mob. I told him that we didn't intend to be lynched. The other policeman who had run around the side of the car started to draw his revolver out of the holster. He was hoping to shoot me in the back. They didn't know that we had more than one gun. One of the students (who was seventeen years old) put a .45 in the policeman's face and told him that if he pulled out his pistol he would kill him. The policeman started putting his gun back into the holster and backing away from the car, and he fell into the ditch.

There was a very old man, an old white man out in the crowd, and he started screaming and crying like a baby, and he kept crying, and he said, "God damn, God damn, what is this God damn country coming to that the niggers have got guns, the niggers are armed and the police can't even arrest them!" He kept crying and somebody led him away through the crowd.

Self-Defense Forces Protection

Steve Presson, who is a member of the Monroe City Council, came along and told the chief of police to open the highway and get us out of there. The chief of police told

10

the City Councilman, "But they've got guns!" Presson said, "That's OK. Open the highway up and get them out of here!" They opened the highway and the man from the City Council led us through. All along the highway for almost a third of a mile people were lined on both sides of the road. And they were screaming "Kill the niggers! Kill the niggers! We aren't having any integration here! We're not going to swim with niggers!"

By the time we got to the pool the other students who had gone on had already started the picket line. There were three or four thousand white people milling around the pool. All the city officials were there, including the Mayor of Monroe. They had dark glasses on and they were standing in the crowd, which kept screaming. Then the chief of police came up to me and said, "Surrender your gun." I told him that I was not going to surrender any gun, that the guns were legal, and that the mob was dangerous; if he wanted those guns he could come to my house and get them after I got away from there. Then he said, "Well, if you hurt any of these white people here, God damn it, I'm going to kill you!" I don't know what made him think that I was going to let him live long enough to shoot me. He kept saying, "Surrender the gun!" while the white people kept screaming.

The City Councilman reappeared and said that the tension was bad and that there was a chance that somebody would be hurt. He conceded that I had a right to picket and he said that if I were willing to go home he would see that I was escorted. I asked him who was going to escort us home. He said "the police." I told him that I might as well go with the Ku Klux Klan as go with them. I said I would go with the police department under one condition. He asked what that was. I told him I would take one of the students out of my car and let them put a policeman in there and then I could rest assured that they would protect us. And the police said they couldn't do that. They couldn't do that because they realized that this policeman would get hurt if they joined in with the mob.

The officials kept repeating how the crowd was getting out of hand; somebody would get hurt. I told them that I wasn't going to leave until they cleared the highway. I also told them that if necessary we would make our stand right there. Finally they asked me what did I suggest they do, and I recommended they contact the state police. So they contacted the state police and an old corporal and a young man came; just two state patrolmen. Three or four thousand people were out there, and the city had twenty-one policemen present who claimed they couldn't keep order.

The old man started cursing and told the people to move back, to spread out and to move out of there. And he started swinging a stick. Some of the mob started cursing and he said, "God damn it, I mean it. Move out." They got the message and suddenly the crowd was broken up and dispersed. The officials and state police knew that if they allowed the mob to attack us, a lot of people were going to be killed and some of those people would be white.

Two police cars escorted us out; one in front and one behind. This was the first time this had ever been done. And some of the white people started screaming "Look how they are protecting niggers! Look how they are taking niggers out of here!"

As a result of our stand and our willingness to fight, the state of North Carolina had enforced law and order. Just two state troopers did the job and no one got hurt in a situation where normally (in the South) a lot of Negro blood would have flowed. The city closed the pool for the rest of the year and we withdrew our picket line.

This was not the end of the story of our struggle in Monroe in 1961. By a quirk of fate the next episode involved the Freedom Riders and their policy of passive resistance. The contrast between the results of their policy and the results of our policy of self-defense is a dramatic object lesson for all Negroes. But before I go on to that I have to describe how our policy of self-defense developed and how the Negro community in Monroe came to support my conclusion that we had to "meet violence with violence."

The story begins in 1955 when, as a veteran of the U.S. Marine Corps, I returned to my home town of Monroe and joined the local chapter of the NAACP.

12

Chapter 2

An NAACP Chapter Is
Reborn in Militancy

My home town is Monroe, North Carolina. It has a population of 11,000, about a quarter of which is Negro. It is a
county seat (Union County) and is 14 miles from the South
Carolina border. Its spirit is closer to that of South Carolina
than to the liberal atmosphere of Chapel Hill which people
tend to associate with North Carolina. There are no trade
unions in our county and the southeastern regional head-
quarters of the Ku Klux Klan is in Monroe.

There was also, at the time of my return from the Marines, a small and dwindling chapter of the NAACP. The
Union County NAACP was a typical Southern branch—small,
not very active, dominated by and largely composed of the
upper crust of the black community—professionals, busi-
nessmen and white-collar workers.

Before the Supreme Court desegregation decision of
1954, the NAACP was not a primary target of segregationists.
In many places in the South, including Monroe, racists were
not too concerned with the small local chapters. But the Supreme Court Decision drastically altered this casual attitude.
The Ku Klux Klan and the White Citizens Councils made it
their business to locate any NAACP chapter in their vicinity
and to find out who its officers and members were. Threats
of violence and economic sanctions were applied to make

13

people withdraw their membership. Chapters, already small, dwindled rapidly.

A Veteran Returns Home

When I got out of the Marine Corps, I knew I wanted to go home and join the NAACP. In the Marines I had got a taste of discrimination and had some run-ins that got me into the guardhouse. When I joined the local chapter of the NAACP it was going down in membership, and when it was down to six, the leadership proposed dissolving it. When I objected, I was elected president and they withdrew, except for Dr. Albert E. Perry. Dr. Perry was a newcomer who had settled in Monroe and built up a very successful practice. He became our vice-president. I tried to get former members back without success and finally I realized that I would have to work without the social leaders of the community.

At this time I was inexperienced. Before going into the Marines I had left Monroe for a time and worked in an aircraft factory in New Jersey and an auto factory in Detroit. Without knowing it, I had picked up some ideas of organizing from the activities around me, but I had never served in a union local and I lacked organizing experience. But I am an active person and I hated to give up on something as important as the NAACP.

So one day I walked into a Negro poolroom in our town, interrupted a game by putting NAACP literature on the table and made a pitch. I recruited half of those present. This got our chapter off to a new start. We began a recruiting drive among laborers, farmers, domestic workers, the unemployed and any and all Negro people in the area. We ended up with a chapter that was unique in the whole NAACP because of working class composition and a leadership that was not middle class. Most important, we had a strong representation of returned veterans who were very militant and who didn't scare easy. We started a struggle in Monroe and Union County to integrate public facilities and we had the support of a Unitarian group of white people. In 1957, without any friction at all, we integrated the public library. It shocked us that in other Southern states, particularly Virginia, Negroes encountered such violence in trying to integrate libraries.

We moved on to win better rights for Negroes: economic rights, the right of education and the right of equal protection under the law. We rapidly got the reputation of being the most militant branch of the NAACP. Obviously we couldn't get this reputation without antagonizing the racists who are trying to prevent Afro-Americans from enjoying their inalienable human rights as Americans. Specifically, we aroused the wrath of the Ku Klux Klan and a showdown developed over the integration of the swimming pool.

The Ku Klux Klan Swings into Action

As I explained in the last chapter, the swimming pool had been built with Federal funds under the WPA system and was supported by municipal taxation. Yet Negroes could not use it. Neither the Federal government nor the local officials had provided any swimming facilities for Negroes. Over a period of years several of our children had drowned while swimming in unsupervised swimming holes. When we lost another child in 1956 we started a drive to obtain swimming facilities for Negroes, especially for our children.

First, we asked the city officials to build a pool in the Negro community. This would have been a segregated pool, but we asked for this because we were merely interested in safe facilities for the children. The city officials said they couldn't comply with this request because it would be too expensive and they didn't have the money. Then, in a compromise move, we asked that they set aside one or two days out of each week when the segregated pool would be reserved for Negro children. They said that this too would be too expensive. Why would it be too expensive, we asked. Because, they said, each time the colored people used the pool they would have to drain the water and refill it.

They said they would eventually build us a pool when

they got the funds. We asked them when we could expect it. One year? They said "No." Five years? They said "No," they couldn't be sure. Ten years? They said that they couldn't be sure. Finally we asked if we could expect it within fifteen years and they said that they couldn't give us any definite promise.

There was a white Catholic priest in the community who owned a station wagon. He would transport the colored youth to Charlotte, N.C., which was twenty-five miles away, so they could swim there in the Negro pool. Some of the city officials of Charlotte saw this priest swimming in the Negro pool and they wanted to know who he was. The Negro supervisor explained that he was a priest. The city officials replied they didn't care whether he was a priest or not, that he was white and they had segregation of the races in Charlotte. So they barred the priest from the colored pool.

Again the children didn't have any safe place to swim at all—so we decided to take legal action against the Monroe pool.

First, we started a campaign of stand-ins of short duration. We would go stand for a few minutes and ask to be admitted and never get admitted. While we were preparing the groundwork for possible court proceedings, the Ku Klux Klan came out in the open. The press started to carry articles about the Klan activities. In the beginning they mentioned that a few hundred people would gather in open fields and have their Klan rallies. Then the numbers kept going up. The numbers went up to 3,000, 4,000, 5,000. Finally the *Monroe Enquirer* estimated that 7,500 Klansmen had gathered in a field to discuss dealing with the integrationists, described by the Klan as the "Communist-Inspired-National-Association-for-the-Advancement-of-Colored-People." They started a campaign to get rid of us, to drive us out of the community, directed primarily at Dr. Albert E. Perry, our vice-president, and myself.

The Klan started by circulating a petition. To gather signatures they set up a table in the county courthouse square in Monroe. The petition stated that Dr. Perry and I should be permanently driven out of Union County because we were members and officials of the Communist-NAACP. The Klan claimed 3,000 signatures in the first week. In the following week they claimed 3,000 more. They had no basis for any legal action, but they had hoped to frighten us out of town by virtue of sheer numbers. In the history of the South in days past, it was enough to know that so many people wanted to get rid of a Negro to make him take off by himself. One must remember that in this community where the press estimated that there were 7,500 Klan supporters, the population of the town was only about 12,000 people. Actually, many of the Klan people came in from South Carolina, Monroe being only fourteen miles from the state border.

When they discovered that this could not intimidate us, they decided to take direct action. After their rallies they would drive through our community in motorcades and honk their horns and fire pistols from the car windows. On one occasion, they caught a colored woman on an isolated street corner and made her dance at pistol point.

At this outbreak of violence against our Negro community, a group of pacifist ministers went to the city officials and asked that the Klan be prohibited from forming these motorcades to parade through Monroe. The officials of the county and the city rejected their request on the grounds that the Klan was a legal organization having as much constitutional right to organize as the NAACP. — SCOTUS case —

Self-Defense Is Born of Our Plight

Since the city officials wouldn't stop the Klan, we decided to stop the Klan ourselves. We started this action out of the need for defense because law and order had completely vanished; because there was no such thing as a 14th Amendment to the United States Constitution in Monroe, N.C. The Local officials refused to enforce law and order and when we turned to Federal and state officials to enforce law and order they either refused or ignored our appeals.

Luther Hodges, who is now Secretary of Commerce, was the Governor of North Carolina at that time. We first

Robert coaching wife Mabel on firearm use and gun safety in Cuba, ca. 1962.

Arms in Perry living room in Monroe, North Carolina. Dr. Perry at right; others from left to right are John H. Williams, Lorraine Williams Garlington, and Edward Williams.

Guards at Dr. Perry's home with odd assembly of weapons.

appealed to him. He took sides with the Klan; they had not broken any laws, they were not disorderly, he said. Then we appealed to President Eisenhower but we never received a reply to our telegrams. There was no response at all from Washington.

So we started arming ourselves. I wrote to the National Rifle Association in Washington which encourages veterans to keep in shape to defend their native land and asked for a charter, which we got. In a year we had sixty members. We had bought some guns too, in stores, and later a church in the North raised money and got us better rifles. The Klan discovered we were arming and guarding our community. In the summer of 1957 they made one big attempt to stop us. An armed motorcade attacked Dr. Perry's house, which is situated on the outskirts of the colored community. We shot it out with the Klan and repelled their attack and the Klan didn't have any more stomach for this type of fight. They stopped raiding our community. After this clash the same city officials who said the Klan had a constitutional right to organize met in an emergency session and passed a city ordinance banning the Klan from Monroe without a special permit from the police chief.

Asian Flu Strikes Schools In Virginia, Carolina

CAROLINA EDITION

Journal and Guide

NORFOLK, VIRGINIA, SATURDAY, OCTOBER 12, 1957

VOL LVII No. 41

20 PAGES   PRICE 15 CENTS

ASIAN FLU--
"What To Do"
Helpful Advice from an Expert
Page 20

CITIZENS FIRE BACK AT KLAN

One of the few papers that covered the attack of the Ku Klux Klan on Dr. Perry's home and the shooting back by defenders. The national press remained silent.

Ku Kluxers Use Guns At Monroe, NC

Shots Exchanged Near Residence Of NAACP Head

Special to Journal and Guide

MONROE, N. C. — It has been reported here that a group of Ku Klux Klansmen, some of them robed and masked, swapped gunfire with a group of colored citizens near the home of the president of the local NAACP branch late Friday night.

Police officials say that no shots were fired, but Union county NAACP Vice-President Robert F. Williams said

fired on a group of some 30 to 40 colored citizens near the home of the NAACP president, Dr. A. F. Perry.

* * *

MR. WILLIAMS also said that when someone in the colored gathering returned the fire, police officers came over to disarm them.

* * *

Police Chief A. A. Mauney has a different version of the affair, however. He says that several police cars were in the caravan of "about 50 cars" that "disbanded" when a train cut across its path. The chief said that he had instructed his men to get in front of the caravan and if any visitations occurred to stop the procession.

* * *

EVEN THOUGH North Carolina law forbids the wearing of masks by adults in public gatherings, Chief Mauney said that he had had reports that some of the Klansmen were hooded.

Police officers in cars in the caravan said that they did hear "what sounded like a carbine near the doctor's house" even though they deny that there was gunfire.

At the time of our clash with the Klan only three Negro publications—the *Afro-American*, the *Norfolk Journal and Guide*, and *Jet Magazine*—reported the fight. *Jet* carried some pictures of the self-defense guard. Our fight occurred two weeks before the famous clash between the Indians and the Klan. We had driven the Klan out of our county into the Indian territory. The national press played up the Indian-Klan fight because they didn't consider this a great threat—the Indians are a tiny minority and people could laugh at the incident as a sentimental joke—but no one wanted Negroes to get the impression that this was an accepted way to deal with the Klan. So the white press maintained a complete blackout about the Monroe fight.

After the Klan learned that violence wouldn't serve their purpose they started to use the racist courts. Dr. Perry, our vice-president, was indicted on a trumped-up charge of abortion. He is a Catholic physician, and one of the doctors who had been head of the county medical department drove forty miles to testify in Dr. Perry's behalf, declaring that when Dr. Perry had worked in the hospital he had refused to file sterilization permits for the County Welfare Department on the ground that this was contrary to his religious beliefs. But he was convicted, sentenced to five years in prison, and the loss of his medical license.

The Kissing Case

In October, 1958, two local colored boys, David Simpson, aged 7, and Hanover Thompson, aged 9, were arrested on the charge of rape which is punishable in North Carolina by death.

This was the famous "Kissing Case." What had happened was that David and Hanover got into a game of "cowboys and Indians" with some white children one afternoon. After a while, the white girls in the group suggested they play "house." One of the little white girls, Sissy Sutton, sat on Hanover's lap and suddenly recognized Hanover as her old playmate. Hanover's mother worked for Sissy's mother and until Hanover reached school age his mother had taken him with her when she went to work at the Sutton house.

When this little girl discovered that Hanover was her old playmate she kissed him on the cheek. Later on in the afternoon she ran home and told her mother how she had seen Hanover and how she was so happy to see him again that she had kissed him.

Sissy's mother got hysterical when she heard this and called the police. Before the two boys had even gotten home they were arrested and thrown into the county jail. If a person is arrested for rape in North Carolina he is not permitted to see anyone for a period of time while the police investigate. Therefore the police didn't notify the boys' parents.

A few days later when we finally found out what had happened and where the two missing boys were, we tried to get help. But the national office of the NAACP wouldn't have anything to do with the case because it was a "sex case." A seven-year-old white girl had kissed a nine-year-old Negro boy on the cheek and the national office didn't want any part of it.

The children were sent to the reformatory soon after they were arrested. I called the civil rights lawyer, Conrad Lynn, and he came down from New York. First thing, he went to talk with Judge Hampton Price, who had passed sentence. The Judge said to Lynn that he had held a "separate but equal hearing." Lynn asked him what he meant by a "separate but equal hearing." And the Judge told him how on the morning of the trial he had called in Mrs. Sutton and her daughter, and Mrs. Sutton had made a statement, and they were sent home. Then in the afternoon the two Negro mothers were summoned to the Judge, and their boys were brought in. Then the Judge said to Lynn, "I told them what Mrs. Sutton had told me and then since they were guilty—I sent them up for fourteen years at the reformatory."

The NAACP national office still wasn't doing anything about the case but an English reporter who was a friend of Lynn's visited the reformatory and sneaked out a photograph of the boys, which appeared along with a story on the front page of the Dec. 15, 1958, *London News Chronicle*. Then

En page 6 : **La leçon des troubles de Léo**

LA GAUCHE

ORGANE   DE   COMBAT   SOCIALISTE

N° 1   1re ANNEE   HEBDOMADAIRE   PRIX : 4 FRANCS   14 JANVIER 1960

Internés pour un baiser !

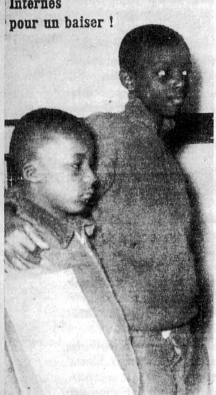

Voir l'article d'Ernest Glinne
en page 5

QUI SEME LE VENT...

LE climat social se détériore rapidement. La réaction multiplie ses coups d'épingles contre le mouvement syndical. Cela irrite les travailleurs. Mais aux coups d'épingles succèdent des attaques contre leur niveau de vie. Et ces attaques ne provoquent pas seulement l'irritation mais la colère.

« Assainissement » des charbonnages ? En refusant d'appliquer un plan de réorganisation d'ensemble, en passant aux fermetures de puits avant que de nouveaux emplois ne soient créés sur place, le gouvernement réactionnaire affirme son intention d' « assainir » aux frais de la classe ouvrière.

« Assainissement » des chemins de fer ? En augmentant les tarifs des abonnements ouvriers en même temps qu'il abaisse les tarifs marchandises et qu'il sape le statut du personnel, le gouvernement précise sa volonté d' « assainir » aux frais de la classe ouvrière.

« Assainissement » des finances de l'Etat ? En augmentant les impôts indirects, impôts antisociaux et antidémocratiques qui pèsent surtout sur les épaules des gagne-petit, le gouvernement confirme sa résolution d' « assainir » aux frais de la classe ouvrière.

« Assainissement » de la sécurité sociale ? En laissant brusquement augmenter de 25 à 35 p.c. les tarifs médicaux, sans augmenter les remboursements, le gouvernement manifeste, sinon sa volonté d'améliorer le fonctionnement de l'assurance maladie-invalidité, du moins son impuissance totale devant l'odieuse rançon que les acolytes du Dr Glorieux imposent à la communauté, profitant d'un monopole de fait et transformant une noble vocation en un bas désir d'enrichissement sans scrupule.

La presse quotidienne l'a déjà précisé : les seules ristournes que l'I.N.S.S. a versé pour frais médicaux en 1957 reviennent à 350.000 fr. par an et par médecin. A quoi s'ajoutent les suppléments touchés, qui s'élèvent au moins à 100.000 fr. par médecin. A quoi s'ajoutent les honoraires touchés des 4 millions de concitoyens non assurés à l'A.M.I. A quoi s'ajoutent les fixes touchés des cliniques et hôpitaux. On voit qu'à part les médecins sociaux et les jeunes, on se trouve en présence d'une caste qui s'enrichit rapidement du malheur des hommes.

Le mauvais coup des médecins est venu au moment où 300.000 ménages belges sont frappés par le chômage, un chômage devant lequel le gouvernement Eyskens se montre complètement impuissant.

Voilà ce qui explique la colère qui monte : des attaques sournoises, le mauvais coup des médecins, le chômage dans lequel s'installe comme dans la plus confortable et la plus normale des situations. Un chômage qui, pour des dizaines de milliers de ménages, réduit les revenus de plus de la moitié, n chômage qu'on fera demain, peser sur les salaires. UN CHOMAGE QUE LES TRAVAILLEURS NE VEULENT PLUS ACCEPTER.

Les organisations ouvrières ont déjà manifesté leur volonté de s'opposer à cette dégradation progressive de la condition ouvrière.

Les aciéries de Cockerill-Ougrée, le lundi 12 janvier, avant de reprendre le travail, ont provoqué spontanément une manifestation à l'intérieur de l'entreprise, passant de division en division, puis parcourant les rues de la commune. Leur manifestation a été suivie d'une prise de position énergique du comité provincial des Métallurgistes liégeois, convoqué d'ailleurs depuis plusieurs jours.

Le collège des organisations mutuellistes belges a dit NON aux médecins.

Les organisations syndicales l'appuyent. Le P.S.B. interpellera le gouvernement.

Comme l'a demandé la semaine dernière la Fédération provinciale de Liège des Métallurgistes, il faut que cette opposition soit organisée, disciplinée, active et efficace.

L'on ne le trompera, en haut lieu, en croyant qu'il s'agit de menaces sur papier, ou de manœuvres électorales. Les organisations ouvrières de ce pays conservent toute leur puissance. Elles sauront la manifester pour défendre leurs affiliés et l'ensemble des travailleurs. La raison demande que chacun prenne au pied de la lettre leurs avertissements.

Sinon, ceux qui sèment le vent risquent de récolter la tempête !

La Gauche

23

all of Europe got wind of the case and there were protest demonstrations in London, Rotterdam, Rome, and Paris. Only then did many American newspapers begin to express "concern" about the "Kissing Case."

At the end of December, 1958, Dr. Perry, Conrad Lynn, and I were called to New York by Roy Wilkins and he offered me a job in Detroit if I'd leave Monroe. I flatly refused his offer.

By now so much pressure was building up abroad and even in the U.S.A. that the NAACP national office entered the case—this case that had until now involved such dreadful sexual implications. In late January there was a hearing, but the children were sent back to the reformatory. Meanwhile, world pressure was mounting. An example is that of the petition signed by the 15,000 students and faculty at a Rotterdam, Holland, high school named after Franklin Delano Roosevelt. The petition called for the release of the children and it was sent to Mrs. Roosevelt.

Somebody said something, finally, to President Eisenhower, and finally he said something to our then Governor Hodges, and on Feb. 13, 1959, the children were released.

"We Will Meet Violence with Violence"

In 1969 Mrs. Georgia White, a Negro mother of five children who worked in a Monroe hotel as a maid, was kicked down a flight of stairs into the lobby of the hotel by a white guest. He said he kicked Mrs. White down a flight of stairs because she had been making too much noise while working in the corridor and had disturbed his sleep. When we asked for an indictment, the chief of police, A. A. Mauney, refused our request. Finally when we threatened to take legal action by bringing in NAACP lawyers, he relented and placed this man under a $75 bond. Even though this white defendant subsequently failed to appear in court for his trial, he was not convicted.

That same day there was another colored woman in court, Mrs. Mary Ruth Reid. Mrs. Reid was eight months pregnant. She was the victim of an attempted rape by a white man who came to her house, drove her from her house, and then beat her. He caught her while she was trying to escape down the main highway and knocked her to the ground. Mrs. Reid's six-year-old boy was running along the side and when the white rapist beat his mother the boy picked up a stick and started hitting the man over the head with it while his mother escaped. She went to a neighbor's house and her neighbor called the police and gave her aid. The neighbor was a white woman and she came to court that day with Mrs. Reid. She came and testified that she had seen the defendant chasing Mrs. Reid and that Mrs. Reid had come to her house in an excited and hysterical state, without shoes, and with her clothes torn from her. This testimony required considerable courage on the part of Mrs. Reid's white neighbor.

During the trial the defense attorney arranged for the defendant's wife to sit at his side as if she were also involved in the case. Then the defense attorney appealed to the jury. He said, "Judge, Your Honor, and ladies and gentlemen of the jury, you see this man. This is his wife. This woman, this white woman is the pure flower of life. She is one of God's lovely creatures, a pure flower. And do you think this man would have left this pure flower for that?" And he made it appear as if the colored woman was actually on trial. Then the defense ended by saying, "It's just a matter of whether or not you're going to believe this woman or this white man. Judge, Your Honor, this man is not guilty of any crime. He was just drinking and having a little fun." The man was acquitted.

Mrs. Reid had several brothers who had wanted to kill her white attacker before the trial began. But I persuaded them not to do anything. I said that this was a matter that would be handled legally, that we would get a lawyer—which we did. We brought a lawyer all the way from New York who wasn't even allowed to take the floor in court. So I was responsible for this would-be rapist not being punished.

The courtroom was full of colored women and when this man was acquitted they turned to me and said, "Now what are you going to do? You have opened the floodgates on us. Now these people know that they can do anything that they want to us and there is no prospect of punishment under law and it means that we have been exposed to these people and you're responsible for it. Now what are you going to say?" I told them that in a civilized society the law is a deterrent against the strong who would take advantage of the weak, but the South is not a civilized society; the South is a social jungle. So in cases like this we have to revert to the law of the jungle; it had become necessary for us to create our own deterrent. I said that in the future we would defend our women and children, our homes and ourselves with our arms. That we would meet violence with violence.

My statement was reprinted all over the United States. What I had said was, "This demonstration today shows that the Negro in the South cannot expect justice in the courts. He must convict his attackers on the spot. He must meet violence with violence, lynching with lynching."

The next day in an interview with the *Carolina Times* I again pointed to the lack of protection from the courts. I said, "These court decisions open the way to violence. I do not mean that Negroes should go out and attempt to get revenge for mistreatments or injustices . . ." I made this statement again on the same day over a Cincinnati radio station. Later that evening in a telecast interview in Charlotte I again made clear that I was speaking of self-defense when the courts fail to protect us.

Since the principle is so obvious, I couldn't understand the commotion my statement aroused or why it should receive so much national publicity. Two years previously, when we had shot up the Ku Klux Klan in self-defense, not a single white newspaper in America reported the incident. We were only serving notice that we would do more of the same, that Negro self-defense was here to stay in Monroe. So I didn't feel we were doing anything new. I realize now that we were establishing a principle, born out of our experience, which could, and would, set an example to others.

Looking back, it is clear that racists made a big error in publicizing our stand. Even though it has caused me and my family a great deal of suffering, the result has been to force a debate on the issue. It also shook up the NAACP considerably out of its timid attitudes and forced an official reaffirmation from the NAACP of the right of Negroes to self-defense against racist violence.

Chapter 3

■ ■

The Struggle for Militancy
in the NAACP

■ ■

Until my statement hit the national newspapers the national office of the NAACP had paid little attention to us. We had received little help from them in our struggles and our hour of need. Now they lost no time. The very next morning I received a long distance telephone call from the national office wanting to know if I had been quoted correctly. I told them that I had. They said the NAACP was not an organization of violence. I explained that I knew that it was not an organization of violence. They said that I had made violent statements. I replied that I made these statements as Robert Williams, not as the National Association for the Advancement of Colored People. They said that because I was an official of the organization anything that I said would be considered NAACP policy, that we were too close together. I asked them why if we were so close together they hadn't come to my rescue all this time when I had been the unemployed victim of the Klan's economic pressure and when I had had all of my insurance canceled as a poor insurance risk. I asked them why they didn't then consider our closeness.

Suspension, Distortion and Re-election

In the next few hours Roy Wilkins of the NAACP suspended me from office. I didn't learn about it from the na-

28

tional office. I first heard of it when Southern radio stations announced and kept repeating every thirty minutes that the NAACP had suspended me for advocating violence because this was not a means for the solution of the race problem and that the NAACP was against Negroes using violence as a means of self-defense.

Our Union County NAACP was one of the few interracial branches in the South. We had some white pacifist members, and when I was suspended they sent a telegram to the national office stating that they were white Southerners and that they were pacifists, but they protested my suspension on the ground that they understood the problems in the community and that the national office did not. This telegram was never made public by the NAACP. And not a single paper ever printed the fact that ours was an interracial branch and that even Southern white pacifists supported my position.

Nevertheless, this all developed into a national debate. We found out that there was no provision in the NAACP consititution to justify or authorize this hypocritical action by Roy Wilkins. I demanded some sort of hearing. Wilkins turned the matter over to the NAACP's paternalistic Committee on Branches, and in New York City on June 3, 1959, they conducted what turned out to be a trial where I fought the suspension. The committee ruled that I was to be suspended for six months' time, after which I would automatically be reinstated.

I didn't think of doing anything more about the suspension; there was a more important matter at hand. As a result of the trial I was more convinced than ever that one of our greatest and most immediate needs was better communication within the race. The real Afro-American struggle was merely a disjointed network of pockets of resistance and the shameful thing about it was that Negroes were relying upon the white man's inaccurate reports as their sources of information about these isolated struggles. I went home and concentrated all of my efforts into developing a newsletter that would in accurate and no uncertain terms inform both Negroes and whites of Afro-American liberation struggles taking place in the United States and about the particular struggle we were constantly fighting in Monroe. The first Issue of *The Crusader* came off the mimeograph machine June 26, 1959.

Then at the last minute I decided to appeal the committee's decision to the NAACP's 50th National Convention which was meeting in New York that July. The national office found it necessary to issue a special convention pamphlet attacking me. This pamphlet tried to confuse my demand that Negroes meet violence with violence as a means of self-defense with the advocacy of lynch law. In its own way the national office contributed to the erroneous impression played up by the racist press that I was agitating for race war and the indiscriminate slaughter of white people.

My suspension was upheld by the convention delegates, many of whom either felt or were pressured into seeing the vote as a question of publicly supporting or disavowing the NAACP national leadership. But on the real issue at hand, delegate sentiment forced the national leadership to support the concept of self-defense. The preamble to the resolutions passed by that convention read, ". . . we do not deny but reaffirm the right of an individual and collective self-defense against unlawful assaults."

While I was suspended, the people in my branch voted to make my wife president to serve in my place. And at the end of the six months, instead of going back into office automatically, I held an election because I didn't want the NAACP national office to think that they were doing me any special favor. We had the election and I was re-elected unanimously.

The national office of the NAACP was determined to keep within the good graces of a lot of the influential Northern whites who were disturbed by our militancy. They maintained an indifferent attitude to our branch. We had a charter and that was all. We were unable to secure assistance from them in any of our school integration cases and our sit-in cases.

In 1960 we started a sit-in campaign. We became the thirteenth town in North Carolina to start sit-in demonstrations. Though the NAACP wasn't taking notice, our sit-ins proved that self-defense and non-violence could be successfully combined. There was less violence in the Monroe sit-ins than in any other sit-ins in the South. In other communities there were Negroes who had their skulls fractured, but not a single demonstrator was even spat upon during our sit-ins. We had less violence because we had shown the willingness and readiness to fight and defend ourselves. We didn't appear on the streets of Monroe as beggars depending upon the charity and generosity of white supremacists. We appeared as people with strength, and it was to the *mutual* advantage of all parties concerned that peaceful relations be maintained.

While the demonstrations were taking place I was arrested and finally sentenced to serve thirty days on the chain gang. The NAACP was supposed to handle my case. They handled it up to the State Supreme Court, but then they dropped my case from appeal without telling me and with only a few days left in which to file an appeal. I discovered this through the newspapers because my case had been consolidated with that of seven students from Chapel Hill, N.C. The newspapers listed the names of the defendants whose NAACP lawyers had filed appeals and I was the only one in the group whose name did not appear. I appealed to the Emergency Civil Liberties Committee. They took my case up and filed an appeal to the U.S. Supreme Court.

"A Letter from De Boss"

All this did not mean that the NAACP national office was short on advice. While they did not feel responsible enough to take the appeal to higher courts, they did feel responsible enough to send me a letter upon my return from Cuba in the summer of 1960. I subsequently made two trips to Cuba.

My experiences in Monroe and with the NAACP which had resulted in launching *The Crusader* were also sharpening my awareness of the struggles of Negroes in every part of the world, how they were treated, their victories and their defeats. It was clear from the first days that Afro-Cubans were part of the Cuban revolution on a basis of complete equality and my trips confirmed this fact. A Negro, for example, was head of the Cuban armed forces and no one could hide that fact from us here in America. To me this revolution was a real thing, not one of those phony South American palace revolutions. There was a real drive to bring social justice to all the Cubans, including the black ones. Beginning late in 1959 I had begun to run factual articles about Cuba in *The Crusader,* pointing up the racial equality that existed there. The articles seem to have stirred up the national office for they sent me a letter which included statements such as these:

".... I wonder, however, whether you are fully aware of the dangers and disadvantages of the course of action you seem to favor. I have followed closely the events in Cuba in recent months and in particular, Dr. Castro's visit to the United Nations this fall. Regardless of the merits of the Cuban cause I was greatly disturbed by the frequent show of insincerity which, I believe, should give you food for thought before you find yourself used as just another pawn in the present unfortunate feud between Cuba and our country.

". . . It is a callous interference in a native American problem and should be recognized as such by anyone in a responsible position of leadership in the American Negro movement.

". . . the present Cuban attempts to endear themselves to American Negroes are obviously caused by ulterior motives. (Let me just ask you how the American Negro tourist would feel in Cuba at the constant chant of 'Cuba si, Yanqui no!')

". . . Are you willing to forsake the important support of that section of the people who are equally opposed to suppression of Negro rights in our country?

". . . Does not the unfortunate example of the great American Negro singer Paul Robeson show you the dangers and mistakes of the road which you seem to be choosing? What has Paul Robeson with all his greatness done for the American Negro in his present struggle for equality: The answer, regrettable as it is, must be: Nothing."

These excerpts were reprinted in *The Crusader* and replied to in this way:

"Only a fool or a mercenary hypocrite could muster the gall to call a nation and its great leader insincere in dealing with the captive blacks of North America when in the course of their daily lives they display the greatest measure of racial equality and social justice in the world today. It is certainly a first magnitude truism that social justice starts at home and spreads abroad. In past months I have twice been to Cuba and there is nothing insincere about my being made to feel that I was a member of the human race for the first time in my life. If this is America's idea of insincerity, then heaven help this nation to become *insincere* like Fidel Castro and Free Cuba in granting persons of African descent entrance into the human race.

"As for my being 'used as a pawn in the struggle of Cuba' against imperialist and racist North America, I prefer to be on the side of right than on the side of Jim Crow and oppression. I prefer to be used as an instrument to convey the truth of a people who respect the rights of man, rather than to be used as an Uncle Tom whitewasher of black oppression and injustice and an apologist for America's hypocrisy. Cuba's aversion for America's inhumanity to man is not an interference in a 'native American problem.' It is common knowledge that the master race of the 'free world' is out to export North American manufactured racism. Racism in the U.S.A. is as much a world problem as was Nazism. If the U.S.A. is to be the only nation exempt from the Human Rights Charter of the United Nations, then that august body is a party to the great transgressions against America's captive people. I, for one, refuse to remain silent and cooperate with the very force that is seeking after my destruction.

"The racists in America are the most brutal people on earth. It is foolhardy for an oppressed Afro-American to take the attitude that we should keep this life-death struggle a family affair. We are the oppressed, it is only natural for us to air our grievances at home and abroad. This race fight in the U.S.A. is no more a fight to be fought just by Americans than is the fight for black liberation to be conducted by colored only. Any struggle for freedom in the world today affects the stability of the whole society of man. Why would you make our struggle an exception?

"I am not afraid of alienating white friends of our liberation movement. If they really believe in freedom they will not resent deviation from the old worn path that has led us in fruitless circles. If they are insincere they are no more than Trojan horses infiltrating our ranks to strike us a treacherous, nefarious blow on behalf of those and that which they pretend to detest. For if they resent our becoming truly liberated, they will detest us for not following their misguidance and skillful subterfuge designed to prevent our arrival to the promised land. They speak much of tolerance, but they display unlimited intolerance toward those Afro-Americans who refuse to become their puppets and yes-man Uncle Toms.

"It is strange that I am asked how a 'Negro' American tourist would feel in Cuba hearing the constant chant of 'Cuba Si, Yanqui No!' No one has bothered to ask how it feels to constantly face 'White Only' signs. These signs mean 'White yes, Colored no!' No one has asked me how it feels to be marched under guard with felons along a public street to jail for sitting on a 'white only' stool. On hearing 'Cuba Si, Yanqui No!' and having lived all of my life under American oppression, I was emotionally moved to join the liberation chorus. I knew it didn't apply to me because the white Christians of the 'free world' have excluded me from everything 'yanqui.'

"You make a cardinal mistake when you fail to give the great Paul Robeson credit for making a great contribution to the American 'Negro' struggle. Paul Robeson is living proof that the Afro-American need not look upon the United States as 'Nigger heaven' and the last stop for us on this earth. Paul is living proof that other civilized societies honor and respect black people for the things that 'Free America' curses, oppresses and starves for. Paul has proven that all black men are not for sale for thirty pieces of silver. He has lit a candle that many of the new generation will follow.

"Yes, wherever there is oppression in the world today,

it is the concern of the entire race. My cause is the same as the Asians against the imperialist. It is the same as the African against the white savage. It is the same as Cuba against the white supremacist imperialist. When I become a part of the mainstream of American life, based on universal justice, then and then only can I see a possible mutual cause for unity against outside interference."

I don't want to leave the impression that I am against the NAACP; on the contrary I think it's an important weapon in the freedom struggle and I want to strengthen it. I don't think they should be worrying about Cuba when there is plenty to worry about in our country. They know, as I know, the extent to which the state governments and the Federal government ignored our appeals for help and protection.

Hypocrisy and Run-around

After we closed the pool, as I've already described, the racists in Monroe went wild. On that same day, after we had gone home, a mob dragged a colored man from his car and took him out into the woods where they beat him, stood him up against a tree and threatened to shoot him. I had called the Associated Press and the UPI and reported that this man had been kidnapped and I also called the Justice Department. Apparently just when this man's attackers were getting ready to shoot him, the chief of police came out and rescued him. How did the chief of police know where to find him in the woods? Later on this Negro was unable to indict anyone who had attacked him even though he recognized some of the members of the would-be lynch mob. The FBI refused to demand any indictments for kidnapping.

The racists would come through the colored community at night and fire guns and we had an exchange of gunfire on a number of occasions. One night an armed attack was led on my house by a sergeant of the State National Guard. He was recognized, but no action was taken against him. And the chief of police denied that an attack had taken place. We kept appealing to the Federal government. It was necessary to keep a guard of about twenty volunteers going every night—men who volunteered to sleep at my house and to walk guard. This was the only way that we could ward off attacks by the racists. The telephone would ring around the clock, sometimes every fifteen minutes, with threatening calls.

Then through my newsletter, *The Crusader,* I started appealing to readers everywhere to protest to the U.S. government, to the U.S. Justice Department; to protest the fact that the 14th Amendment did not exist in Monroe and that the city officials, the local bureau of the FBI in Charlotte, and the Governor of the state of North Carolina were in a conspiracy to deny Monroe Negroes their Constitutional rights.

One of the readers of *The Crusader* wrote to Congressman Kowalski of Connecticut, who in turn wrote a letter to the Attorney General, Robert Kennedy. He said that he had been appalled to learn about the lawlessness in Monroe, and how this was damaging to our country at a time when the United States was claiming to be a champion of democracy in the world. The Congressman asked for an investigation. But despite all those letters and telegrams to the U.S. Justice Department, no investigation was made. The only investigation they made was to ask our chief of police if these things were true. The chief of police assured them that they were not.

Finally I went to the Charlotte bureau of the FBI and filed a long report calling for a Federal indictment of the chief of police for denying citizens their rights guaranteed by the 14th Amendment. This report was filed, but I never heard from the FBI. Later a newspaperman told me that he had heard from the Justice Department and that they claimed they could find no evidence of any violation of the 14th Amendment in Monroe. They never did bother to answer me.

Yet it was at this time that I received a letter from the United States Department of State. In this letter they denied my family and me the right to travel to Cuba, where we had been invited for the 26th of July celebration. The grounds for their refusal were: "because of the break in diplomatic relations between the United States and Cuba, the government of the United States cannot extend normal protective services to its citizens visiting Cuba."

This false pretense of being interested in protecting me was a farce of the first magnitude and classic hypocrisy. Numerous threats and four attempts of murder had been made on my life in the preceding three weeks and the would-be assassins, aided and abetted by local officials, were offered immunity from law by the deliberate silence of Federal officials to whom I had continuously appealed for "normal protective services." The Federal government couldn't possibly have been interested in protection for me and my family, for they passed up many opportunities to protect us here at home.

This all happened a month before I was forced to leave Monroe.

Chapter 4

■ ■

Non-Violence Emboldens the
Racists: A Week of Terror

■ ■

In our branch of the NAACP there was a general feeling that we were in a deep and bitter struggle against racists and that we needed to involve as many Negroes as possible and to make the struggle as meaningful as possible. We felt that the single issue of the swimming pool was too narrow for our needs, that what we needed was a broad program with special attention to jobs, welfare, and other economic needs.

I think this was an important step forward. The struggles of the Freedom Riders and the Sit-In Movements have concentrated on a single goal: the right to eat at a lunch counter, the right to sit anywhere on a bus. These are important rights because their denial is a direct personal assault on a Negro's dignity. It is important for the racists to maintain these peripheral forms of segregation. They establish an atmosphere that supports a system. By debasing and demoralizing the black man in small personal matters, the system eats away the sense of dignity and pride which are necessary to challenge a racist system. But the fundamental core of racism is more than atmosphere—it can be measured in dollars and cents and unemployment percentages. We therefore decided to present a program that ranged from the swimming pool to jobs.

The Monroe Program

On Aug. 15, 1961, on behalf of our Chapter I presented to the Monroe Board of Aldermen a ten point program that read as follows:

PETITION

We, the undersigned citizens of Monroe, petition the City Board of Aldermen to use its influence to endeavor to:

1. Induce factories in this county to hire without discrimination.
2. Induce the local employment agency to grant non-whites the same privileges given to whites.
3. Instruct the Welfare Agency that non-whites are entitled to the same privileges, courtesies and consideration given to whites.
4. Construct a swimming pool in the Winchester Avenue area of Monroe.
5. Remove all signs in the city of Monroe designating one area for colored and another for whites.
6. Instruct the Superintendent of Schools that he must prepare to desegregate the city school no later than 1962.
7. Provide adequate trasportation for all school children.
8. Formally request the State Medical Board to permit Dr. Albert E. Perry, Jr., to practice medicine in Monroe and Union County.
9. Employ Negroes in skilled or supervisory capacities in the City Government.
10. ACT IMMEDIATELY on all of these proposals and inform the committee and the public of your actions.

(signed)

Robert F. Williams
Albert E. Perry, Jr., M.D.
John W. McDow

Our demands for equal employment rights were the most important of the ten points. Many plants were moving in from the North—runaway industry from the North moving in to avoid labor unions, seeking low-priced workers in the South. They received considerable tax-supported concessions from the local Industrial Development Commission and they didn't hire any Negroes. In fact, local bigoted officials had done everything in their power to prevent Negroes from obtaining employment. They had even gone so far as to stipulate that the new industries could not hire Afro-Americans if they expected the special concessions made possible through the taxation of us all. This amounted to taxation without representation and it was one of our biggest complaints.

As a result of this racist policy, out of approximately 3,000 Afro-Americans in Monroe, there are 1,000 unemployed—persons unable to obtain jobs even as janitors, maids, or porters. And maids and porters, when employed, earn at most $15 for a six-day week. One of the few kinds of work available, cotton picking, pays all of $2.50 for 100 pounds of picked cotton; at breakneck speed it takes a long day, much more than eight hours, to pick 150 pounds. Virtually every Negro high school and college graduate in Monroe has to leave to find employment. This is not true of the white graduates. Negroes are even laid off in the summer so white college youth can work at home. Meanwhile, each summer our street corners are crowded with colored youths just out of school. They have no means of gainful employment or wholesome recreation.

For reasons such as these we believe that the basic ill is an economic ill, our being denied the right to have a decent standard of living.

The Freedom Riders Come to Monroe

We had planned to put picket lines around the county courthouse to draw attention to our program and to apply pressure for its achievement. At this time seventeen Freedom Riders came to our support, perhaps the first time that they engaged in a struggle over such fundamental demands as our program presented. Hitherto, as I've said, the goals were peripheral and while important, amenable to small compromises. For example, we had won integration in the public library. On these peripheral matters, leaders of the Sit-In Movements can meet with city and state officials and win concessions. I believe this is an important part of the overall Negro struggle. But when these concessions are used for propaganda by Negro "leaders" as examples of the marvelous progress the Afro-American is supposedly making, thereby shifting attention from the basic evils, such victories cease to be even peripheral and become self-defeating. When we tackle basic evils, however, the racists won't give an inch. This, I think, is why the Freedom Riders who came to Monroe met with such naked violence and brutality. That and the pledge of non-violence.

The Freedom Riders reflected an attitude of certain Negro leaders who said that I had mishandled the situation and that they would show us how to get victory without violence. With them came the Reverend Paul Brooks, sent by the Reverend Martin Luther King, Jr., to act as a "troubleshooter" for the Freedom Riders, should the need arise, and to work with the community, helping it to develop nonviolent techniques and tactics. I disagreed with their position but was more than willing to co-operate. The community rented a house for them which was christened "Freedom House" in their honor. They were joined by some of our militant youth who had participated in the picket lines around the swimming pool the previous month. Together they formed the Monroe Non-Violent Action Committee.

Although I myself would not take the non-violent oath, I asked the people of the community to support them and their non-violent campaign. Monroe students took the non-violent oath, promising to adhere to the non-violent discipline, which, along with other principles, prohibited self-defense. I also stated that if they could show me any gains won from the racists by non-violent methods, I too would become a pacifist.

At the same time, several observers were in Monroe to see for themselves what so-called democracy was like in Union County. We knew that people living in other sections of the country and other countries of the world would find it hard to believe that such vicious racist conditions, such

brutality and ruthlessness, existed in the United States especially in such a "progressive" Southern state as North Carolina was supposed to be. So we encouraged these visits.
Julian Mayfield, the young Afro-American novelist and an old
friend of Monroe, was there. A young exchange student, Constance Lever of Durham, England, was a guest at our house
along with Mrs. Mae Mallory, who had been active in the
movement for true integration in her own city, New York.

When the Monroe Non-Violent Action Committee set up
its picket line on the first day, the Freedom Riders seemed
convinced they were making real progress. One Freedom
Rider even returned from the line overjoyed. He said, "You
know, a policeman smiled at me in town today while I was
on the line." I laughed and told him not to pay that any attention because the policeman was probably smiling at the
thought of how best to kill him. Constance, the English exchange student, had joined the picket line. She said, "Oh, I
don't think these people are so bad. I just think you don't
know how to approach them. I noticed that they looked at
me in a friendly way in town today." I tried to explain to her
that these people were trying to win her and the others over
in the hope that they would leave Monroe. The day that
these people realized that they couldn't win the Freedom
Riders over, they would show their true nature. A few days
later, Constance Lever was arrested by the Monroe police
and charged with "incitement to riot."

The Racists Act by Violence

It was on the third day that the townspeople started
insulting the pickets and their politeness turned to vicious-
ness. A policeman knocked one picket to the ground and
threatened to break his camera. Another was arrested and
all the time the white crowd heckled. When one of the white
Freedom Riders smiled back at the hecklers, two of Monroe's "pure white flowers" spit in his face. Tensions continued to mount.

On the fourth day a white Freedom Rider was attacked

on the street in town and beaten by three whites. The police broke this up and promised to arrest the white people who had attacked this Freedom Rider. So the Freedom Riders kept on thinking there was a possibility that the law would be on their side because they had publicly proclaimed themselves to be non-violent. I told them it was all right for them to be pacifists but they shouldn't proclaim this to the world because they were just inviting full-scale violent attack. In the past we hadn't had any victims of the type of violence they were beginning to experience because we had shown a willingness to fight. We had had picket lines and sit-ins and nobody had successfully attacked our lines. But they said they were struggling from a moral point of view.

On Friday a white Freedom Fighter was shot in the stomach with a high-powered air rifle as he was walking the line. This happened right in front of the police. And that day the city sprayed the picket line with insecticide, hoping to drive the students away from the line. Meanwhile, the city had passed special laws, ordering pickets to be fifteen feet apart at all times. They had to maintain this distance; they couldn't be too close or too far apart. Then the police started using the tactic of stopping one picket and when the one behind continued walking on they would arrest him for passing too closely behind the other. Also that afternoon, a Negro boy, ten years old, was attacked in town by three white men because he had been seen on the picket line. None of the attackers was arrested.

"Ain't You Dead Yet?"

That night the Freedom Riders went for a ride into Mecklenburg County across the line and stopped at a restaurant. There they were recognized and attacked by white racists. In the scramble one of the Freedom Riders could escape only by running into the woods; the others had to flee in the car, leaving him behind. We notified the Monroe city police, our county police, the Charlotte police, and the Mecklenburg County police that a Freedom Rider was in the woods, missing, and the racists were trying to catch him. We were afraid he would be lynched. We asked them to intercede. The Monroe police refused. The Union County police refused.

Rev. Brooks called the Governor's office. Governor Terry Sanford was out, they said. But Rev. Brooks got an opportunity to speak to the Governor's chief aide, Hugh B. Cannon, and complained to him about the lack of police protection for the Freedom Riders. The Governor's aide kept talking about Robert Williams. Rev. Brooks said he was not calling about Robert Williams; he was calling about a missing Freedom Rider. He said that they were pacifists, non-violent people, and wanted police protection. The Governor's aide, Hugh B. Cannon, replied, "If you're a real pacifist you had better get the hell out of Monroe, man, because there's going to be plenty of violence there."

Rev. Brooks kept trying to appeal to him for police protection but finally gave up. He said, "Since you're talking about Robert Williams so much, he's right here. Do you want to talk to him?" The Governor's aide said, Yes.

Cannon and I had talked about two weeks before when I had asked for state police protection. Instead the Governor had sent an Uncle Tom representative named Dr. Larkins, who is supposed to be the Governor's troubleshooter. He came and held a secret meeting with me to find out what it would take to quiet things down. I gave him the ten-point program and it shocked him. He said that it was too much, that the demands were too high, but he would take it up with the Governor anyway. And he said that, well, he understood I had been undergoing economic pressure and that this was wrong and that maybe I could get a job, that maybe the state could help me if we just didn't start any trouble around here.

When I called back the Governor's office and told Hugh B. Cannon about this bribe attempt, he replied, "You mean to tell me that you're not dead yet?" And I told him, "No, I'm not dead, not yet, but when I die a lot of people may die with me." So he said, "Well, you may not be dead, but you're going to get killed." I kept telling him that we wanted protection, trying to avoid bloodshed. He said, "If you're trying to avoid bloodshed you shouldn't be agitating."

The Governor and the FBI

So this Friday night, when Rev. Paul Brooks finished talking to Hugh B. Cannon and he said he wanted to talk to me, I got on the phone and told him what had happened. He said, "Well, you're getting just what you deserve down there. You've been asking for violence, now you're getting it." I told him that I wasn't appealing to him for myself. I was appealing to him for a pacifist. And I told him, "Besides, I'm not appealing to you for a Negro; this happens to be a white boy who's lost in the woods." He said, "I don't give a damn who he is. You asked for violence and now you're getting it, see; you're getting just what you deserved." So I told him, "Do you know one thing . . . you are the biggest fool in the whole world!" He became infuriated and started raging on the telephone and told me to shut up. I told him that he may be the Governor's assistant but he couldn't tell me to shut up. He said, "If you don't stop talking to me like that I'll hang up." And he finally hung up. No protection came.

Each time the Freedom Riders would get ready to go on the picket line they would call the FBI in Charlotte and ask for protection. The FBI would say, "We're on our way." But they would never be there when anything happened. On Saturday when the Freedom Riders were picketing in town and the taxicabs that had been transporting them to the line had started out to pick them up, the local white racists gathered together and blocked the road. This meant the Freedom Riders had to walk back to the colored community which was almost a mile away. The mob followed the Freedom Riders along the streets, throwing stones at them and threatening to kill them. When they came into the colored community, the colored people who were not participating in the picket line became very upset that our community had been invaded by a mob chasing Freedom Riders. Many of the colored people started stoning cars and beating back the white racists.

Chapter 5

■ ■

Self-Defense Prevents a Pogrom: Racists Engineer a Kidnapping Frameup

■ ■

Sunday morning the chief of police and his men drove through the county urging whites to come to town to fight the Freedom Riders. In addition, people were coming in from other counties and from South Carolina. An organization called the Minute Men had brought people in.

By afternoon thousands of white racists had gathered in town, concentrating at the courthouse square. At 4 o'clock James Forman, one of the picket captains, called my home requesting four taxicabs within the hour. He said that the racists were threatening to assault the line and complained of police indifference. Forman was to end up in jail with a split head one hour later.

At 4:30 the Negro cab company called to report that they couldn't get through to the picketers because every entrance into town was blocked off. Minutes later a couple of cars driven by our people came racing into the neighborhood. They had just made it in from town to report that the mob had started to attack the picket line, shots had been fired and the town was in the grip of a full-scale riot.

When the self-defense guard, which up to now had stayed away from the courthouse square, heard that the lives of the Freedom Riders and local non-violent youth were in danger, they jumped into their cars and rode into town, breaking through the mob's blockade to rescue the picketers. Julian Mayfield went with them.

The white mob was already armed. The police disarmed some of the men attempting to rescue the Freedom Riders and turned these additional weapons over to the mob. Firing broke out at the picket line when the police and the mob tried to prevent the English exchange student from getting into one of the rescue cars driven by three armed Negroes. The police held Negroes while white racists beat them up. At first the victims were all Freedom Riders and the local non-violent students, but soon Negroes were attacked indiscriminately as the mob fanned out all over town. They were massing for an attack against our community.

We Aim for Self-Defense

So many Freedom Riders and Negroes were arrested that many prisoners with legitimate charges against them were released from jail to make room. Many of these people who came out of jail reported to me that students were bleeding to death there without any medical attention. I called the chief of police and told him that I had reports that the students were not getting medical attention and that their lives were in danger. I told him I would give him just thirty minutes to get medical attention for them and that if they didn't receive medical aid within thirty minutes, we would march on the jail. About fifteen minutes later James Forman called from the hospital to let me know that they were receiving medical care. Just after that, Julian Mayfield returned and reported that members of the white mob, which now included some uniformed police, were near the railroad tracks and firing down at Negroes who had fled town. At the approach of darkness, white people started driving through our community, shouting and screaming. Some fired out of their cars and threw objects at people on the streets. Many of the colored people started arming, exchanging guns, borrowing ammunition and forming guards for the night to defend the community from the mob massing in town. On the block where I live there were about 300 people milling around the street.

About 6 o'clock in the evening a white couple, Mr. and Mrs. Bruce Stegall, came riding through our neighborhood. They were recognized as people who had driven through town the day before with a banner on their car announcing an "Open Season On Coons." It meant that this was killing time.

People have asked why a racist would take his wife into a riot-torn community like ours on that Sunday. But this is nothing new to those who know the nature of Klan raiding. Many Southern racists consider white women a form of insulation because of the old tradition that a Negro is supposed to be intimidated by a white woman and will not dare to offend her. White women are taken along on Klan raids so that if anything develops into a fight it will appear that the Negro attacked a woman and the Klansman will of course be her protector. Mrs. Stegall was brought along as insulation by her husband. They were trying to see what defenses we were preparing for that night.

The Negroes out on the street were raging. Some of them had been beaten in town. Some of their children were missing and some children were in jail. As soon as the Stegalls' car entered our street it was recognized and stopped at gunpoint less than a block away from my house. I was in the house at the time receiving telephone calls from all over town: calls from parents crying about their children who had participated in this demonstration; calls from Negroes reporting that they were beaten and asking what should be done, what action to take; calls from Negroes volunteering to fight, Negroes offering to join in armed groups so they could defend the community. When I wasn't on the phone I was out in the back of my house setting up a defense line before nightfall.

When the Stegalls were stopped, they were taken out of their car and brought into my yard. Someone called me out of the house and I came out and saw all these people milling around the Stegalls. I realized how angry these people were and I saw the circle closing in around the Stegalls. I knew that if just one person lost control of himself the Stegalls would be killed. I started driving the crowd away from them, forcing the crowd out of reach.

Then Mrs. Stegall said, "We've been kidnapped!" She kept repeating this. I said, "Lady, you're not kidnapped. You can leave when you get ready but you got to go through this crowd and these people are angry." She stood up and looked at the crowd and she said, "You should take us out of here. You could take us out. If you took us out of here they wouldn't bother us." I said, "Lady, I didn't bring you here and I'm not going to take you away. You knew that all these people would be here; you know how rioting has been going on in the town and you should have known better than to come into a place like this where the people are angry and upset like this. We are too busy now trying to defend our homes. I'm trying to set up a defense line and I don't have time to bother with you. That's your problem."

While we were standing there talking, an airplane flew over us. The airplane probably was either from the Klan or the Sheriff's Department. They use plenty of light planes and we were constantly getting calls threatening to bomb us from the air since my house was too well guarded to get us from the ground. So when this plane swooped over the house about fifteen men armed with high-powered .30-caliber rifles opened fire. Mrs. Stegall had been very indignant and arrogant, but as soon as she saw this she realized how serious the situation was, that these people were angry and really meant business. She started shaking all over and almost became hysterical. Then a car with white men drove by, firing, and about twenty fellows fired back and you could see flames where the bullets struck the car. Mrs. Stegall could see this.

I started into the house and the crowd began screaming that the Stegalls should be killed. When I started walking up the front steps Mrs. Stegall was right up against me, walking right up against my body and her husband was right up against her. They followed me on into the house while all these people were still screaming that they should be killed.

One man was begging for somebody to give him a gun and let him, please, let him kill them.

Some of the people in this crowd I had never seen before. Negroes were coming from out of the county, they were coming from other towns or calling long-distance on the telephone offering to join in the defense group that was being formed. But all the people who had been regularly affiliated with me and in the guard were in the back of my house because that was where we were assembling and checking out our weapons and ammunition for the night. The street crowd consisted of Negroes who had become angry and involved. They didn't belong to any organization, to any one group. They were just armed private citizens who were fed up with oppression.

I went to the telephone and my wife gave the Stegalls a seat. When I came back the woman kept repeating, "If you'll take us out of here we'll be all right." And I told her again that I didn't have time to take her out. I told her that if I had been caught in her community under similar conditions I would already be dead. I said, "You see, we are not half as cruel as your people." And she admitted that I was right. She told me that she was a church-going Christian and that she wanted to help us and she wished there was something she could do. And I told her that her husband could help us. And he said he didn't know what he could do since he wasn't well known around Monroe, that they lived in Marshville. She kept saying, "*You're* Robert Williams!" and I told her, "Yes." She said, "Well, I never met you before, but I heard a lot of talk about you." And I said, "It was all bad." And she said, "Yes, I must admit that it was all bad, but you're not the type of fellow they say you are. You seem to be a good fellow. You're much better than I thought."

The telephone rang again. It was the chief of police, A. A. Mauney. He said, "Robert, you've caused a lot of race trouble in this town, but state troopers are coming. In thirty minutes you'll be hanging in the courthouse square."

He hung up. Someone else called and said there was a news flash on television that troops were being sent to surround the town. Another woman called and said that she

50

saw troops moving in and that the highway patrol was parking its cars behind the jailhouse. This was confirmed by a radio flash. Then one of our fellows called me to the door. I went out into the street and looked around. Both ends were being blocked off by police cars. I realized they were trying to trap me into waiting until the state troopers got there. I told Mabel, my wife, that we had to leave. I said she didn't have time to take anything, just to get the children. I called Julian Mayfield who had left just after the Stegalls followed me in, and told him about the state troopers moving in around my area, advising him to leave Monroe immediately so that if something happened to me, someone would be free to tell the world the story. Then we left.

In Flight But Not a Fugitive

Most people think that we left because we were fleeing an indictment. But the possibility of an indictment hadn't even occurred to me at that time. Remember, I left Monroe knowing I had *saved* the lives of the Stegalls. We were fleeing because of the attitude of the state, because of the attitude of the chief of police, because of the *lack* of law. We didn't learn about the indictment until we were in New York and heard it flashed on radio and television. When we left North Carolina we headed directly for New York. In the beginning I thought that we would stay there; that we would stop over in Harlem and from there we would immediately start a campaign to tell the world about the ruthless racist oppression that was taking place in Monroe. It was for this reason that I had left North Carolina. Only from outside the state could I organize a publicity campaign that would bring help to the Negroes and Freedom Riders so hopelessly outnumbered in Monroe. I had left North Carolina only after the chief of police had called me and told me that the state troopers were coming and that in thirty minutes I would be hanging in the court house square. I remembered the words of Hugh B. Cannon when I had appealed to him for protection under law for the missing Freedom Rider. The Governor's aide told me

51

that he didn't give a damn about anyone, that we had asked for violence and now we were going to get it. He wanted to know then "why I wasn't dead yet!" I didn't think then that anything legal was involved.

The first I knew of the indictment was in New York when I heard over the radio that there was an all-points alarm out for me and that I had been indicted for kidnapping the Stegalls by the Union County Grand Jury.

The FBI claims that it entered the case because I was an indicted fugitive from justice in interstate flight to avoid prosecution. But technically the FBI is wrong, because I left Monroe early that night—about 9 o'clock. When the grand jury indicted me sometime late the next day, I was already in New York. I certainly didn't cross the North Carolina state line as an indicted fugitive.

But this technical error in the Federal charge that was made against me so that I might be "legally" hounded throughout the whole United States is not at all surprising when one thinks of the complete falsity of the state kidnapping charge. It is very important to note what happened immediately after I left Monroe. I was indicted on the testimony of two policemen (there is no court record that the Stegalls ever appeared before the grand jury). Then, with the warrant issued, my house was raided by about a hundred officials of the state, the Federal government, and the local police armed with machine guns, rifles, riot-guns and tear gas. They didn't know that I had already left. They couldn't believe that I had got away.

When I read about the grand jury indictment in the New York papers, it was accompanied by interviews of reporters with Mrs. Stegall. I don't know what Mrs. Stegall finally told the grand jury, if she ever did appear before them. But I do know she couldn't keep her story straight for the reporters and she never told the same version twice.

I read stories in *The New York Post* and *The New York Times* the following day reporting that when they had questioned Mrs. Stegall she said that I had chided the crowd for kidnapping her and her husband. Yet she turned around in the next paragraph and said that I was responsible because

I was the ringleader of these people. Next I read that she claimed that they had been tied up in my house and held at gunpoint and that when I left the house they were still there. But after saying that they were tied up, then she turned around and said that they were released by me unharmed and left an hour and a half later.

Meanwhile, she was claiming various reasons for being in the colored community in the first place. In one paper she said they were taking a short cut. For another paper she said that they were lost, that they didn't know where they were going. But no highway runs through our community. This was a dead-end street almost a mile from the highway that the Stegalls would use to get back to Marshville. Any person who knew the county could not possibly get lost there. The Stegall woman also told one reporter that the house I lived in, the house that I was born in, had been sold to my father by her father and that she had once lived there herself. In all these stories it was always Mrs. Stegall doing the talking and Mrs. Stegall's picture that you saw. They never had Mr. Stegall, who was a known Klansman, saying anything.

I also read a report where Mrs. Stegall was quoted by the *Charlotte Observer* as saying "that Williams only pretended that he was trying to help us." Well, how would she know? One of the best proofs that I was helping them is the fact that they were unharmed and still alive. And they know this.

Chapter 6

■ ■

The Monroe Case:
Conspiracy against the Negro

■ ■

What has happened and continues to happen in Monroe, N.C., illustrates an old truth: that words used in common by all men do not always have a meaning common to all men. Men have engaged in life-or-death struggles because of differences of meaning in a commonly-used word. The white racist *believes* in "freedom," he *believes* in "fair trial," he *believes* in "justice." He sincerely believes in these words and can use them with great emotion because to the white racist they mean his freedom to deprive Negroes of their basic human rights and his courts where a "fair trial" is that procedure and "justice" that decision which upholds the racist's mad ideal of white supremacy. On many desperate occasions when our constitutional rights were denied and our lives were in danger, we called on the Justice Department and the FBI to investigate the Monroe situation, to protect our lives and to restore our constitutional rights—in other words, *to administer justice*. And they always refused our request.

The Department of Justice—
"Extremely Dangerous and Schizophrenic"

The U.S. Justice Department is showing itself as abetting the conspiracy in Monroe against Negroes by the Ku

54

Klux Klan. After we had left Monroe the U.S. Justice Department, in collaboration with the chief of police, A. A. Mauney, released 250,000 "wanted" circulars. In these circulars they describe me as "schizophrenic." In describing me as schizophrenic they do not say who had psychoanalyzed me. Do they mean I was analyzed as being schizophrenic by Monroe's semi-illiterate chief of police?

The Justice Department released these vicious posters describing me as "extremely dangerous." But they failed to cite any substantiating facts. They failed to cite any criminal record. They failed to cite any cases that could justify this charge. They failed to tell what harm I had ever done to anyone. This was because they knew that these things were lies. Now, how could the Justice Department of the United States do this? How could it mean well? How could it be an impartial investigative body, spreading such vicious lies throughout the United States without any investigation of the facts, without investigating the source of these malicious lies?

In their posters were such "facts" as that I had a scar over my right eye, a scar to the left of my nostril and a scar on my left leg. All of this is untrue, but these ridiculous lies about nonexistent scars helped to create a picture of the "razor-fighting nigger," of someone "extremely dangerous." All this means that the U.S. Justice Department has joined forces with the Ku Klux Klan. They were so sure that I would not escape that they were prematurely justifying what they considered was going to be a legal lynching at the behest of the United States government. They had said I would not hesitate to shoot. This was to justify someone shooting me if I had been taken into custody.

When I fled to Canada they also passed these same posters on to the Royal Canadian Mounted Police. And in Canada, interestingly enough, they never mentioned the fact that race incidents had occurred in North Carolina, or that the only crime that I was guilty of was the crime of fighting for human rights in the South. There is plenty of proof of this. Since the sit-in demonstrations started in the South, over 5,000 Negroes have been arrested for struggling for their rights. Almost all of the militant leaders in the South have spent some time in jail for no more than asking for their Constitutional and human rights.

The Justice Department was afraid that the Canadians, who are not as prejudiced as white Americans, would understand what this case was really all about and refuse to cooperate. They had to make it appear—and this is the work of the United States government through its agency, the U.S. Justice Department—that I was a common criminal who had kidnapped for ransom. They created the impression that I was hiding in Canada and was heavily armed.

Again the question is: *Where did this information come from?* Did the U.S. Justice Department go to the same chief of police that I had asked them to indict? The same chief of police against whom I had filed an affidavit? The same chief of police that they knew had been my enemy and the enemy of Negroes and a friend of the Ku Klux Klan since 1956? Did they go to a Klan-sponsored chief of police to ask him for data on a United States civil rights fighter? Well, they most certainly did. And this should be enough to awaken many people to the fact that the Justice Department of the United States is itself contaminated by racist influences.

If I had not been able to escape from the United States I would never have gotten to a trial, let alone a fair trial.

The Other Defendants

Mrs. Stegall reported that my home was an "armed camp." But the raid on my house had failed to produce any trace of these arms or ammunition. So the police used my disappearance as an excuse to raid through the rest of the community; tearing up homes, terrorizing a lot of the people who weren't even in the defense guard, grilling in all-night sessions persons known to be my associates, and confiscating the weapons they found—weapons we possessed legally.

The Freedom Riders who were out of jail said that although I was gone they were going to carry on the struggle; they would carry on this fight that we had started. They made this statement to *The New York Post* and to *The New*

York Times a day after I left. One of them was John Lowry, a twenty-year-old white college student from New York. Two days after he declared that the struggle would be continued he was arrested and charged with complicity. Richard Crowder, a local nineteen-year-old youth who had been elected chairman of the Monroe Non-Violent Action Committee, was also indicted along with seventeen-year-old Harold Reape. These boys had participated in the original picket line and in the sit-in demonstration and they had shown leadership ability in this struggle. Therefore they were indicted for complicity. Mae Mallory, who left North Carolina after the rioting started, was also charged with complicity, but no immediate attempt was made to apprehend her.

In addition, Albert Rorie (seventeen years old) and Jimmie Covington (fifteen years old), two other local Negro youth who had participated in all of these struggles, were each charged and indicted with having shot a policeman apiece, although the City of Monroe never could produce more than one wounded policeman. Jimmie Covington was committed to reform school. Albert Rorie was given five years in prison. This case is pending on appeal to the state Supreme Court.

Richard Griswold of Brooklyn, New York, another white Freedom Rider arrested during the rioting on the 27th, was beaten almost to the point of death in the Union County jail that day by another prisoner, a white criminal being held on forgery and assault charges. Griswold's life was saved only because another arrested Freedom Rider was led past the cell in which Griswold was lying, blood-covered and semi-conscious. The second Freedom Rider, Kenneth Shilman, started yelling at the top of his lungs, demanding that Griswold be removed from the cell before he was killed. The warden complied because he thought the white student would die and then there would really be trouble.

Starting the very next day, all the different city, county, state, and Federal law-enforcement agencies began sending each other telegrams about how law and order had been reestablished in Monroe. And the week following the riots each employee of the Sheriff's Department was awarded $100 extra pay by the Board of County Commissioners. The bonus was "compensation for special services rendered during the 'race emergencies' in Monroe."

Almost three weeks later The Committee to Aid The Monroe Defendants (CAMD) received a handwritten, signed confession from Howard Stack, the white prisoner who had been Griswold's cellmate. Stack admitted that he had beaten Griswold at the behest of the Monroe police who had prom-

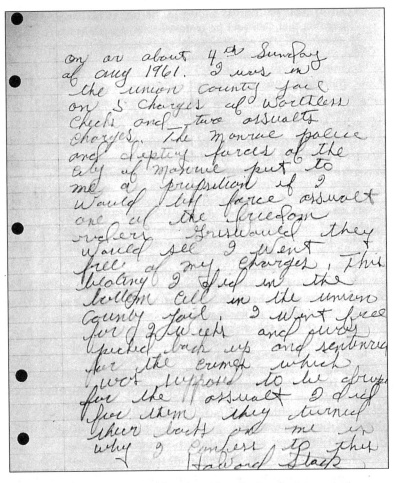

Handwritten confession of Howard Stack that he beat up the young Freedom Rider Griswold at the behest of Monroe police. This confession was sent to the Department of Justice, which took no action.

58

ised to drop the charges against him and release him immediately in exchange for the beating. Stack sent this confession to the CAMD because two weeks after he was released he was again picked up and sentenced on the same charges that were supposedly dropped.

Conrad Lynn forwarded the original of the confession to Attorney General Robert Kennedy and asked for an immediate investigation of the Monroe Police Department. The Justice Department never acknowledged receiving the confession. FBI agents did come around and secure depositions and even interviewed Stack. Meanwhile, Union County authorities quickly committed Stack to a mental institution and the Justice Department notified Lynn finally that their file was closed.

The Spectre of the Russian Rifles

Soon various newspapers in the United States began to report statements by local police officials that when they raided our community they discovered and seized our secret armory: *Russian rifles with sickle and hammer insignia.* They implied that these weapons were supplied by some sort of ominous international Communist conspiracy. The insinuation was that of a secret weapons cache shipped to us directly by Moscow. This was a pure smear. They suppressed the information that many of our rifles were of *various* foreign makes. They failed to mention that we had British surplus rifles with the insignia of the Crown. Why didn't they recognize that we were agents of the Queen, hoping to restore the monarchy in America? Nor did they mention our rifles of Italian manufacture. They failed to mention that we also had German rifles with Nazi insignia. These were World War II weapons, Mausers. They didn't think it important to mention that we had such weapons. Or possibly they approve of rifles with Nazi insignia. They also failed to mention that we had surplus rifles from the United States Army, the M-1 rifle with U.S. Army insignia. Why didn't they try to involve us in a conspiracy with the U.S. Army?

cold war paranoia

They mentioned only the rifles of Russian origin in order to smear our self-defense movement. It was a tactic to arouse hysteria among the racists and to mislead the American people. It was an attempt to inject fake emotional issues of the Cold War into our fight for survival. It was an attempt to make the American people think that the Monroe self-defense movement was a grave threat to their security.

The plain fact is that these rifles can be bought in army-navy surplus stores and regular hardware stores throughout the United States. These rifles were purchased legally, including the Russian rifles with the hammer and sickle insignia. I received signed bills of sale with the numbers of these Russian rifles on them.

This was no special secret supply or hidden armory. We had a rifle club with a charter from the National Rifle Association since 1957. We were authorized to have rifles. We did target practice. There are three other gun clubs in Monroe, three white gun clubs. The white people even have two segregated professional rifle ranges. But not a single newspaper mentioned any of these facts.

Newspapers like *The New York Post* started crying and sobbing hysterically about Russian rifles being found, but they failed to mention that these rifles were bought openly in stores in the United States. These Russian rifles were not automatic weapons. They were the bolt-action type used for sport and marksmanship firing and had won five out of six trials in the Olympics of 1959. This rifle is called the 6.53 and it is not even used in the Russian Army. The "Russian rifles" smear was perpetrated by sensationalist journalists who somehow didn't see anything at all sensational when policemen armed white thugs to attack non-violent students in Monroe.

I have a picture taken from a recent issue of the *Toronto Star* of members of the so-called U.S. Minute Men, the fascistic organization that is in fellowship with the John Birch Society. The photograph shows the Minute Men in training in the state of Illinois. Not the state of Mississippi, not the state of Alabama or South Carolina, but the state of Illinois. These people are equipped with machine guns and automatic rifles, including the Johnson automatic rifle, and they are firing U.S. Army 6.5-mm. mortars. They are firing these mortars on prepared ranges and firing live ammunition. Where did they get these mortars? Where did they get this ammunition? No surplus stores in the United States sell mortars or live shells. Where did they get their machine guns and automatic rifles, many models of which still are in use by the United States Armed Forces? Unlike our weapons, automatic rifles and machine guns may not be owned by civilians. This is specified by Federal law.

These men are wearing standard steel helmets and are dressed in surplus uniforms of the U.S. Army. The only difference is that they have their own Minute Men insignia. These men have raised and mobilized their own private army. Some of the 5,000 men recruited in Monroe to attack the Freedom Riders were components of this fascistic Minute Men organization.

Nobody was upset about this. None of these pious-sounding newspapers, so interested in the welfare and the security of the American people, breathed a word about Minute Men being brought into Monroe. These Minute Men have been arming and training with heavy weapons in the field. What is the reason for this? Why has this been tolerated in the United States? The Minute Men say that they are mobilizing to fight Communism or possible invasion of the United States by the Communists. Wouldn't an American be naive indeed to believe that if the United States Marine Corps, the Infantry, the Navy, and the Air Force couldn't stop some sort of invasion, how in the hell could a few old women in tennis shoes from the John Birch Society and their corps of Minute Men stop them?

Anyone who can think logically can see that the racist Minute Men are being armed and prepared for pogroms. They are becoming a fascist vanguard that will some day be turned loose on all Afro-Americans and white Americans who get out of line. And to get out of line means to petition militantly for Constitutional rights. These Minute Men types will be the people who do the dirty work. Just as there were special units to man the gas furnaces for the Jewish people

America as an Apartheid State.

61

in Nazi Germany, so "special units" will develop to handle "trouble-makers" in a fascist America. This must be done outside of the jurisdiction of the armed forces because the U.S. Armed Services are integrated. But the Minute Men organizations are not integrated. It will be like the French Army and the O.A.S. in Algeria. They will look the other way, like the Wehrmacht and the S.S. corps in Hitler's time. The Armed Services of the United States, the police officials, the Justice Department will look the other way and say, "We're sorry, but we can't catch these people. We're sorry, but we've done everything we can do to prevent violence." The Minute Men have pure, 100 per cent, all-American weapons and the newspapers have barely found cause to denounce their activities.

But when the Negroes of Monroe, outnumbered and outarmed, gallantly rose to defend their homes, their families, and their persons, their efforts at self-defense were scorned by the press and they were smeared with the insinuation that their weapons were furnished by some insidious Communist conspiracy.

All the American people, not just Afro-Americans, must realize that if we had not been armed in this city of Monroe, Union County, North Carolina last August 27, there would have been mass bloodshed. There is only one reason why the racist mob lost its nerve in their projected attack on the Negro community. Knowing as they did that we were well armed, they found it impossible to stomach the thought of violence.

These are people who would like to do violence to others but want to have immunity from violence themselves. They are the people who just love it when pacifist Negroes turn the other cheek.

Our preparations and constant armed vigilance to protect our homes from attack were completely divorced from the campaign of the Freedom Riders and our local students who were picketing and demonstrating on a non-violent basis. *We armed ourselves solely to defend ourselves.* And if we hadn't been armed, we would have been the victims of one of the first modern pogroms against the Afro-American.

Let the newspapers wail and bemoan about our rifles with Communist insignia. I don't care what kind of insignias the rifles had on them. They were a godsend to us that Sunday, August 27, 1961.

Canada—Then Cuba

When I realized that this was no longer a local matter and that the U.S. Government had entered into the picture and was just as determined to destroy me as the Ku Klux Klan, I decided that I had to leave New York and that the best place to go would be Canada.

I felt that the Canadian people would be sympathetic. I also remembered that Canada had been a place of refuge for escaped Negroes using the underground railway during the time of slavery in the United States. So I made my way on to Canada with my wife Mabel. I felt secure in Canada. For a few days I lived a normal life. I went around town shopping— window shopping. I attended an air show and went to the park and to the beaches. It seemed to me that I was quite secure. I felt that there was a possibility that I would be able to remain in Canada since charges against me were really trumped up.

One morning, to my surprise, there was a huge picture of me on the front page of a Canadian newspaper. The story that went with the photo said that I was a vicious kidnapper and that the Justice Department of the United States had appealed to the Royal Canadian Mounted Police to apprehend me. It referred to me as a laborer and freight handler. It didn't mention that I was president of the Union County branch of the National Association for the Advancement of Colored People. Nor did it mention that I had written, edited, and published a newsletter.

The Royal Canadian Mounted Police initiated a search that was just as vicious and carried out just as energetically as the FBI search. Since there were many Canadians who realized what the race situation was in the United States and who sympathized with me, the Royal Canadian Mounted Police started searching homes. They even searched a church in Toronto (and questioned the minister) where I had appeared while on a speaking tour the previous summer. I decided that Canada would be no safer than the United States. I had made plans with sympathetic Canadians to fight extradition proceedings if I was apprehended in Canada. They were prepared to show that the authorities were trying to return me to the violence, brutality, and racial oppression of the South, and they had hired lawyers for me in Canada who were ready to take immediate legal action in the event of my arrest. But luckily I was able to leave Canada.

When I realized that I would not be safe in Canada, I remembered my two trips to Cuba. I could think of no other place in the Western Hemisphere where a Negro would be treated as a human being, where the race problem would be understood, and where people would not look upon me as a criminal but as a victim of a trumped-up charge—a charge designed to crush the militant leaders who were beginning to form a new movement, a new militant movement designed for the total liberation of the Afro-Americans.

Since all the eastern coast of Canada was being watched by the FBI and the Royal Canadian Mounted Police, I traveled across Canada to the west coast, re-entered the United States and made my way into Mexico and from there to Cuba. That was why I came to Cuba—because I had no alternative.

The Complicity of the Ohio Governor

Shortly after Cuba announced that she had granted me political asylum, Mrs. Mae Mallory was arrested by agents of the FBI in Cleveland, Ohio, where she had gone for asylum. The state of North Carolina immediately requested that she be extradited back to Union County to stand trial.

If Mrs. Mallory is extradited, she will join Lowry, Reape, and Crowder and be tried on a yet undetermined date in a North Carolina court, where there is no possible chance of their obtaining justice, especially under the conditions that

Robert F. Williams at a press conference with the Cuban Bar Association, March 1962.

I've described. Much pressure is building up throughout the country. Many people are preparing to protest this great miscarriage of justice because these indictments carry life-time sentences in prison.

When Mrs. Mallory was first arrested in Cleveland considerable protest occurred in Ohio. Responding to this pressure by the Afro-American community, the Rev. Martin Luther King Jr. signed a Monroe Defense Committee petition

THE CRUSADER

MONTHLY NEWSLETTER

ROBERT F. WILLIAMS, Editor —IN EXILE—

VOL. 3 — No. 8   APRIL 1962

Truth Crushed to Earth Shall Rise Again

IT has truly been said that "truth crushed to earth shall rise again." True to this adage, the fighting little CRUSADER Newsletter returns to the vanguard of the

CUBA: Territorio Libre de América

liberation struggle. Yes, it yet lives to haunt those who thought they had destroyed it. THE CRUSADER with its editor in exile is going to be a monthly printed journal. It

asking Gov. Michael DiSalle not to extradite Mae Mallory. Mrs. Mallory was granted an executive hearing and two months later Gov. DiSalle made his decision. It was to extradite Mrs. Mallory back to Monroe.

Despite thousands of petition signatures, telegrams, and letters of protest from trade unions, civil liberties organizations, and civic groups not only in Cleveland but throughout the country, Gov. DiSalle made this decision and refused to reverse it. Gov. DiSalle justified his decision on the basis of two telephone conversations with North Carolina's Gov. Terry Sanford, who "assured" Gov. DiSalle that "Mrs. Mallory would receive a fair trial in a North Carolina court."

Does this great liberal Governor of Ohio really believe Negroes can secure justice in North Carolina courts just because the Governor of that state assured him that such justice exists? North Carolina is a state where a Negro man was convicted and sentenced to five years in prison because it was said that he leered at a white woman, that he looked at her too attentively. Despite the fact that he was 75 feet away, he was still convicted in a state superior court and sentenced to five years.

This is also a state where just two years ago a seventeen-year-old Negro girl was beaten to death in prison by a guard because she complained about the bad prison food. The state entered into a settlement with her parents. They paid her parents $1,900 as a settlement for having killed their daughter.

Evidently this is Gov. DiSalle's concept of "assured" justice for Negroes. Does he find even more reassuring the instances of so-called North Carolina "justice" that have occurred since the August frame-ups?

This is a state where in early fall, while Gov. DiSalle was talking over the phone with Gov. Terry Sanford and "carefully examining the North Carolina record in administered justice," a young girl, a Negro teen-ager, raped by four white men she could positively identify, was unable to obtain justice from any North Carolina law enforcement agency. When she went to the Marshville police, the Union County sheriff's office, and finally to the FBI and told them that she had been raped, giving them the names of the men who had raped her, all refused to do anything about it. The local FBI office refused because they said this was a local matter. Then finally, when the pressure from the Negro community threatened to become explosive, one of the men was charged, brought to trial, and in five minutes acquitted.

In this same state, just weeks after Gov. DiSalle made his decision to extradite Mae Mallory, a twenty-year-old Negro was convicted of rape and sentenced to ten to twenty years in prison. Despite the fact that the white woman involved repeatedly asserted in court that it was not he who had raped her, the white jury brought in their verdict of guilty. They did this because they knew that the accused and the woman had been long-time friends—something these people cannot tolerate.

At the same time, in this same state, North Carolina, in this same city, Monroe, another Negro youth, held incommunicado for twenty days on three trumped-up charges, was shot in the leg by a policeman when he attempted to escape from the dungeon cell in which he was being kept in solitary confinement—the same cell in which Richard Griswold was so brutally beaten. No North Carolina attorney would represent this boy, Jayvan Covington. Finally, two young Washington, D.C., lawyers volunteered their services as counsel only a week before the trial was scheduled, but the court refused them more time to prepare the defense. Jayvan Covington was found guilty of three felony charges and was also convicted on two misdemeanors: resisting arrest—he wanted to know what he had been arrested for—and attempted escape. He was sentenced to seven to ten years on these charges. When an appeal was filed, a $15,500 bond was sent pending appeal. So Jayvan Covington is still in his cell and recently has been threatened with an extra charge of "secret assault" if he goes through with his appeal.

This is the same law, the same court that set bail at $2,000 for a white man, a known member of the Klan, who was charged with murder, charged with killing a Negro man by shooting him in the back of the head. This white man doesn't even deny the shooting; he claimed he had caught the Negro peeping into a local joyhouse. A week prior to this, another Negro was shot in the hip and is in serious condition. Yet he is in jail unable to raise the $8,000 bail while the white man who shot him is free—claiming he shot the Negro for attempting to break and enter, or for peeping. The Monroe court hasn't decided yet what to call it so it will sound most believable at trial.

This is North Carolina, the state where the second highest official in the government expressed surprise that I was still alive when we appealed to him for no more than enforcement of law and order. This is what Governor Sanford would like to have Mae Mallory return to. This is the type of justice in store for the Negro youth who are now facing trial there, and for John Lowry.

The Mallory case reminds us once more that no Afro-American is out of the reach of Klan justice so long as he is on soil presided over by racists. It is an indictment of American justice to have a Northern state collaborate with the South in a legal lynching. The Mallory case proves that even a Northern state like Ohio helps the racists. Terry Sanford knows that he can depend on a fellow Democrat like DiSalle to return fugitive slaves.

concept that even the Northis entrenched by racism

To the World: "Take Note of Monroe"

On a date to be fixed after Mae Mallory is returned to North Carolina, my co-defendants will be brought to trial in a Monroe, North Carolina, courtroom. Only an aroused and outraged world opinion can possibly save them from the frame-up fate that the authorities have planned. Only an attentive world opinion, sharply focused on that Monroe courtroom, can possibly restrain the racist authorities.

We are asking the world to take note of Monroe, to register its indignation and shock that a government which proclaims itself leader of the "free world" persecutes its freedom-fighting youth.

We have started a world-wide campaign for signatures

to a petition which will be presented to the Human Rights Commission of the United Nations. It demands an immediate international investigation into the denial of human rights in Monroe. We are asking labor organizations, human rights committees and student organizations all over the world to join in this protest.

Our one hope for the Monroe defendants is that the United States will be civilized enough and responsive enough to be mindful that the whole world is disgusted with its treatment of the Afro-American. We hope that the pressure of world resentment will force the U.S. government to give them justice regardless of their race, regardless of their role as freedom fighters, and regardless of their dissent in a racist system, and that they will be restored to the decent society of people who believe in social justice.

This is not a new tactic. World protest saved two young boys from fourteen-year reformatory sentences in the Monroe "Kissing Case." In 1960, when the Monroe city officials drafted an "urban renewal plan" calling for Federal "slum clearance" funds to condemn and destroy the houses of the colored community, we telegraphed a protest-appeal to honorary NAACP member Jawaharlal Nehru, who at that moment had President Eisenhower as his guest in India. The Federal Housing Administration subsequently refused to approve the Monroe project. In 1961, after the Cuban invasion fiasco, when President Kennedy justified U.S. intervention for "the cause of freedom," we sent an open telegram (read at the United Nations) to the President requesting equivalent U.S. tanks, airplanes, artillery, machine guns, and mercenary troops to fight the Klan in North Carolina.

The only difference now is that we will mobilize opinion on a larger scale. When the racists forced me into exile they unwittingly led me onto a greater field of battle.

This is the time for demonstrations like the one we had in the United Nations protesting the lynching of Patrice Lumumba. We must display the type of courage that will embarrass this nation before the world. All this time we will further identify our struggle for liberation with the struggle of our brothers in Africa, and the struggle of the oppressed of Asia and Latin America. They in turn will further identify their struggle with ours. The U.S. government is powerful enough to eliminate racial discrimination overnight. But it tolerates and abets Jim Crow.

This government will increasingly discover that every discriminatory action against Afro-Americans it tolerates or abets will be understood as a crime against their brothers by the "uncommitted" colored peoples it so wishes to influence.

Chapter 7

■ ■

Self-Defense:
An American Tradition

■ ■

The stranglehold of oppression cannot be loosened by a plea to the oppressor's conscience. Social change in something as fundamental as racist oppression involves violence. You cannot have progress here without violence and upheaval because it is a struggle for survival for one and a struggle for liberation for the other. Always the powers in command are ruthless and unmerciful in defending their position and their privileges. This is not an abstract rule to be meditated upon by Americans. This is a truth that was revealed at the birth of America and has continued to be revealed many times in our history. The principle of self-defense is an American tradition that began at Lexington and Concord.

Minds Warped by Racism

We have come to comprehend the nature of racism. It is a mass psychosis. When I have described racial conditions in the United States to audiences of foreign newsmen, Cubans and other Latin Americans, they have been shocked to learn of the depths of American race hatred. When I have cited as illustrations such extreme situations as the segregation of telephone party-lines in Union County or the segregated pet-animal cemetery in Washington, D.C., where an Afro-American cannot bury his dog, they find such things comic as well as pathetic.

Such extreme examples of the racist mentality only appear comic when looked upon as isolated phenomena. In truth they are perfectly logical applications of the premises that make up the racist mentality. Look at the phenomena this way and they are the logical inventions of a thoroughly diseased mind. The racist is a man crazed by hysteria at the idea of coming into equal human contact with Negroes. And this mass mental illness called racism is very much a part of the "American Way of Life."

When Afro-American liberation is finally achieved in the U.S.A., one of the many new developments in such a society will be some sort of institution that will correct those Americans whose minds are thoroughly warped by racism. Somehow a way will be found so that these insane people will be made whole and well again.

"We Must Create a Black Militancy . . ."

This is the time for the Afro-American to act. Our sense of national consciousness and militancy is growing. I speak of the masses of people, the masses of Afro-Americans that I know and have visited: in Jacksonville, Florida; in Atlanta, Savannah and Macon, Georgia; in Columbia, Charleston and Greenville, South Carolina. The oppressed and exploited black men that I've met on the streets of Harlem, on the streets of Detroit, and in Chicago. And I speak of the people in Monroe where five years ago, when I started talking about self-defense on the street, many of my black neighbors would walk away to avoid me. Today, despite the FBI manhunt and my exile, despite the frame-up arrests and the shootings since, despite the intimidation campaigns like the one to drive Mrs. Johnson of *The Crusader* staff from Monroe, despite all this, black Monroe continues its struggle.

As editor of *The Crusader,* I went south in the fall of 1960, deep into Jim Crowland, to observe the freedom struggle. I was confronted with this new wonderful spirit rising throughout Dixie—this determination to break the chains of bondage and the spirit of valor of a people who just a few years ago were submissive peons in civilization's no-man's-land. Daily I saw the old myth about Afro-Americans being incapable of unity and action exploded.

In Savannah an NAACP leader contributed $30,000 to the local branch. The branch has a full-time worker and a suite of office space. Pickets and sit-iners have been beaten and jobs have been lost, but the struggle goes on. The leader is not afraid of violence to himself because the people are with him. In that city an Afro-American union leader said that it had come to pass that the masses of Afro-Americans can see that "We must defend ourselves against violence with violence." Many of them now say that the American white racist needs a good "whipping" to bring him down to earth and to break his white supremacy mania.

I learned in Atlanta that Mr. Elijah Muhammed had made quite an impression and that many Afro-Americans are learning, to the consternation and embarrassment of the black respectable leadership, that he has more to offer than weak prayers of deliverance. A prominent minister in South Carolina said, "Our biggest stumbling block is the Uncle Tom minister—the people must stop paying these traitors." In Atlanta a university professor, energized by the new spirit on the part of the Negroes, was very hopeful that new militant leadership would replace the old Uncle Toms whose days, he was confident, were numbered.

There are exceptions among us. The Uncle Toms, the Judases, and the Quislings of the black "elite" would deny this rising consciousness. They do everything possible to make white Americans think that it is not true, while apologizing for us to the very people who oppress us. Some of these "responsible" Negroes are afraid that militant action damages "amiable race relations." They complain that race relations may deteriorate to a point that many Negroes may lose jobs. What they mean is that they may lose *their* jobs. For the black workers, who are the first to be fired and last, if ever, to be hired, the situation is so bad it can't deteriorate.

We realize that there must be a struggle within our own ranks to take the leadership away from the black Quislings who betray us. Then the white liberals who are dumping hundreds of thousands of dollars into our struggle in the South to convert us to pacifism will have to accept *our* understanding of the situation or drop their liberal pretensions.

Why do the white liberals ask us to be non-violent? We are not the aggressors; we have been victimized for over 300 years! Yet nobody spends money to go into the South and ask the racists to be martyrs or pacifists. But they always come to the downtrodden Negroes, who are already oppressed and too submissive as a group, and ask them not to fight back. There seems to be a pattern of some sort of strange coincidence of interest when whites preach a special doctrine to Negroes. Like the choice of theology when the plantation-owners saw to the Christianization of the slaves. Instead of the doctrines which produced the rugged aggressively independent and justice-seeking spirit that we associate with Colonial America as the New England Conscience, the slaves were indoctrinated in the most submissive "trust-your-master," "pie-in-the-sky after-you-die" form of Christianity.

It is because our militancy is growing that they spend hundreds of thousands of dollars to convert us into pacifists. Because our militancy is growing they come to us out of fear.

Of course, the respectable Negro leadership are the most outspoken exponents of non-violence. But if these people, especially the ministers, are such pure pacifists, why is it that so few, if any, criticize the war preparations of this country? Why is it that so few speak out against the Bomb? Isn't that the sort of preaching one expects and *hears* from sincere pacifists? The responsible Negro leadership is pacifist in so far as its one interest is that we do not fight white racists, that we do not "provoke" or enrage them. They constantly tell us that if we resort to violent self-defense we will be exterminated. They are not stopping violence—they are only stopping defensive violence against white racists out of a fear of extermination.

This fear of extermination is a myth which we have exposed in Monroe. We did this because we came to an active understanding of the racist system and grasped the relationship between violence and racism. The existence of violence is at the very heart of a racist system. The Afro-American militant is a "militant" because he defends himself, his family, his home and his dignity. He does not *introduce* violence into a racist social system—the violence is already there and has always been there. It is precisely this unchallenged violence that allows a racist social system to perpetuate itself. When people say that they are opposed to Negroes "resorting to violence" what they really mean is that they are opposed to Negroes defending themselves and challenging the exclusive monopoly of violence practiced by white racists. We have shown in Monroe that with violence working *both* ways constituted law will be more inclined to keep the peace.

When Afro-Americans resist and struggle for their rights they also possess a power greater than that generated by their will and their hands. With the world situation as it is today, the most racist and fascist United States government conceivable could not succeed in exterminating 20,000,000 people. We know there is a great power struggle going on in the world today and the colored peoples control the true balance of power. We also know, from the statistics of the Detroit race riots, that production in this country would fall in forty-eight hours. People everywhere in the world would be ready to support our struggle.

Nor should we forget that these same deceiving pacifist-preaching well-to-do southern blacks profit from the struggle, living lives of luxury while most Afro-Americans continue to suffer. Are they any better than the Negro Quisling in neighboring Charleston, North Carolina—a black man who rode around in a new pink Cadillac with anti-NAACP and anti-integration literature, a huge roll of money and an expense account, all the blessings of the White Citizens' Council? It is an ironic sign that black Judases are becoming more expensive as the white racist becomes desperate—

though it is small consolation to those of us who suffer from his betrayals.

In Monroe, where we fought the Klan, we were being penalized. There are children there growing up without any education, children without shoes, children without food. Old people without medical attention. For the Monroe Negro, there is no work; there is no welfare. From all the money raised in the North by the official black leadership, no one would send a penny to Monroe because the white liberals who gave this money considered us to be outlaws and thugs. They preferred to let us suffer rather than to identify themselves with our position. They sent truck convoys into other places in the South but penalized us because we took a militant stand.

But our children who are growing up without shoes are also growing up with a sense of direction they cannot obtain in the Jim Crow schools. There once was a threat, in Monroe, of Negro teen-age gang war. It abated as the teen-agers resolved their difficulties by coming to understand the problem. It is only natural to expect the black youth to be infected with a desire to do something. Frustrated by less active adults, this desire may be projected in the wrong direction. The vigor of the youth can be channeled into constructive militant actions. It is simply a matter of common sense to have these young Negroes constructively fight racial injustice rather than fight among themselves. Danger is not a respecter of color lines. It is better to bleed for a just cause than to bleed just for the thrill of the sight of blood. Rebellion ferments in modern youth. It is better that it expend itself against its true enemies than against teen-age schoolmates who can't even explain the reasons for their dangerous skirmishes.

The Montgomery bus boycott was perhaps the most successful example of completely pacifist action. But we must remember that in Montgomery, where Negroes are riding in the front of buses, there are also Negroes who are starving. The Montgomery bus boycott was a victory—but it was limited. It did not raise the Negro standard of living. It did not mean better education for Negro children, it did not mean economic advances.

Just what was the issue at hand for the white racists? What sacrifice? Remember that in Montgomery most white Americans have automobiles and are not dependent on the buses. It is just like our own experience in Monroe when we integrated the library. I called the chairman of the board in my county. I told him that I represented the NAACP, that we wanted to integrate the library, and that our own library had burned down. And he said, "Well, I don't see any reason why you can't use the same library that our people use. It won't make any difference. After all, I don't read anyway." Now, this is the attitude of a lot of white Southerners about the Montgomery bus boycott. The white people who control the city didn't ride the buses anyway. They had their own private cars, so it didn't make any difference to them.

But when Afro-Americans get into the struggle for the right to live as human beings and the right to earn the same amount of money, then they'll meet the greatest amount of resistance, and out of it will come police-condoned or inspired violence. When that happens, the racist must be made to realize that in attacking us he risks his own life. After all, his life is a white life, and he considers the white life to be superior. So why should he risk a superior life to take an inferior one?

I believe, and a lot of other Negroes do too, that we must create a black militancy of our own. We must direct our own struggle, achieve our own destiny. We must realize that many Afro-Americans have become skeptical and extremely suspicious of the so-called white liberals who have dominated "Negro" freedom movements. They just feel that no white person can understand what it is like to be a suppressed Negro. The traditional white liberal leadership in civil rights organizations, and even white radicals, generally cannot understand what our struggle is and how we feel about it. They have always made our struggle secondary and after all these years we really never got any place.

They have a patient sense of good public relations. But we're not interested in a good press. We're interested in becoming free. We want to be liberated. To me oppression is harmful. It is painful. I would wake up in the morning as a Negro who was oppressed. At lunchtime, I would eat as a Negro who was oppressed. At night I would go to bed as a Negro who was oppressed. And if I could have been free in thirty seconds, it would not have been too soon.

"Too long have others spoken for us," began the first editorial in the first Afro-American newspaper, which began publication in 1827. The truth of these words has not dimmed in the century and a half since they first appeared in *Freedom's Journal*. They are more appropriate than ever.

There are white people who are willing to give us aid without strings attached. They are willing to let us direct our own struggle. They are genuinely interested in the liberation of the Negroes. I would not have been able to remain in the South as long as I did if it had not been for the support that I got from some white people in the North. And I might never have succeeded in escaping the legal-lynching manhunt fomented by the FBI or have reached Cuban sanctuary but for the help of whites. They will be willing to continue helping us for the sake of justice, for the sake of human decency.

[handwritten margin note: white allies are indispensable to equality]

"Every Freedom Movement in the U.S.A. Is Labeled 'Communist' "

I am not a member and I have never been a member of the Communist Party. But most decent-minded Americans should realize by now that every movement for freedom that is initiated in the United States; every movement for human dignity, for decency, every movement that seeks fairness and social justice, every movement for human rights, is branded as "Communistic." Whenever a white person participates in a movement for black liberation, the movement is automatically branded as "under the domination of Moscow." I can't expect to be an exception.

This Communist-thing is becoming an old standard. An old standard accusation now. Anyone who uncompromisingly opposes the racists, anyone who scorns the religious fanatics and the super-duper American conservatives is considered a Communist.

This sort of thing gives the Communists a lot of credit because certainly many people in my movement in the South don't know what a Communist is. Most of our people have never even heard of Marx. When you say Marx some of the people would think that maybe you were talking about a fountain pen or a New York City cab driver. Or the movie comedians.

But people aspire to be free. People want to be liberated when they are oppressed. No matter where the leadership comes from. The enslavement and suppression of Negroes in the American South were going on before Karl Marx was born, and Negroes have been rebelling against their oppression before Marxism came into existence. As far back as the 16th century, and the beginning of the 17th century, Negroes were even rebelling on the slave ships. The history of American Negro slavery was marked by very many conspiracies and revolts on the part of Negroes.

Certainly the Marxists have participated in the human rights struggle of Negroes, but Negroes need not be told by any philosophy or by any political party that racial oppression is wrong. Racial oppression itself inspires the Negro to rebellion. And it is on this ground that the people of Monroe protested and on this ground that the people of Monroe refused to conform to the standard of Jim Crow life in a Jim Crow society. It is on this basis that they have struck out against the insanity of racial prejudice. We know that the Southern bigot, the Southern racist is mentally ill, that he is sick. The fact that Jim Crow discrimination and racial segregation may very well be based on economic exploitation is beside the point.

We are oppressed and no matter what the original cause or purpose of this oppression, the mind and personality of the racist doing the oppressing have been warped for so long that he is a mental case. Even if the economic situation is changed it will take quite a while and require quite a shock to cure this mental disease. I've read that one of the best treatments for some forms of mental illness is the shock treatment. And the shock treatment must come primarily from the Afro-American people themselves in conjunction with their white allies, in conjunction with the white youth. This movement that I led was not a political organization. It had no political affiliations whatsoever. It was a movement of people who resented oppression. But I would say one thing about our movement. What happened in Monroe, North Carolina, had better become a lesson to the oppressors and the racists of America. Because it is symbolic of a new attitude, symbolic of a new era. It means that the Negro people are becoming restless. It means that there will be many more racial explosions in the days to come. Monroe was just the beginning. I dare predict that Monroe will become the symbol of the new Afro-American, a symbol of the Afro-American determined to rid himself of the stigma of race prejudice and the pain and torture of race hate and oppression at any cost.

Black Nationalism: Another Label

The label "Black Nationalist" is as meaningless as the Communist label. The Afro-American resents being set aside and oppressed, resents not being allowed to enter the mainstream of American society. These people who form their own groups because they have been rejected and start trying to create favorable societies of their own are called "Black Nationalists."

This is a misleading title. Because the first thing you must remember is that *I* am an Afro-American and *I've* been denied the right to enter the mainstream of society in the United States. As an Afro-American I am rejected and discriminated against. We are the most excluded, the most discriminated-against group in the United States; the most discriminated-against class. So it is only normal that I direct most of my energy toward the liberation of my people, who are the most oppressed class.

As for being a "Black Nationalist," this is a word that's hard to define. No, I'm not a "Black Nationalist" to the point that I would exclude whites or that I would discriminate against whites or that I would be prejudiced toward whites. I would prefer to think of myself as an *Inter-Nationalist*. That is, I'm interested in the problems of all mankind. I'm interested in the problems of Africa, of Asia, and of Latin America. I believe that we all have the same struggle, a struggle for liberation. Discrimination and race hatred are undesirable, and I am just as much against racial discrimination, in all forms, every place in the world, as I am against it in the United States.

What do we mean by "nationalism"? When you consider the present white American society it can be classified as nothing but a nationalistic society based on race. Yet as soon as an Afro-American speaks out for his people and is conscious and proud of his people's historical roots and culture, he becomes a "nationalist." I don't mind these labels. I don't care what they call me. I believe in justice for all people. And because the Afro-American is the most exploited, the most oppressed in our society, I believe in working foremost for his liberation.

Non-Violence and Self-Defense

The tactics of non-violence will continue and should continue. We too believed in non-violent tactics in Monroe. We have used these tactics, we've used all tactics. But we also believe that any struggle for liberation should be a flexible struggle. We should not take the attitude that one method alone is the way to liberation. This is to become dogmatic. This is to fall into the same sort of dogmatism practiced by some of the religious fanatics. We can't afford to develop this type of attitude.

We must use non-violence as a means as long as this is feasible, but the day will come when conditions become so pronounced that non-violence will be suicidal in itself. The day is surely coming when we will see more violence on the American scene. The day is surely coming when some of the same Negroes who have denounced our using weapons for self-defense will be arming themselves. There are those who pretend to be horrified by the idea that a black veteran who shouldered arms for the United States would willingly take up weapons to defend his wife, his children, his home and his life. These same people will one day be the loud advocates of self-defense. When violent racism and fascism strike at their families and their homes, not in a token way but in an all-out bloody campaign, then they will be among the first to advocate self-defense. They will justify their position as a question of survival. When it is no longer some distant Negro who is no more than a statistic, no more than an article in a newspaper, when it is no longer their neighbors but them, and when it becomes a matter of personal salvation, then their attitude will change.

As a tactic we use and approve non-violent resistance. But we also believe that a man cannot have human dignity if he allows himself to be abused, to be kicked and beaten to the ground, to allow his wife and children to be attacked, refusing to defend them and himself on the basis that he's so pious, so self-righteous, that it would demean his personality if he fought back.

We know that the average Afro-American is not a pacifist. He is not a pacifist and he has never been a pacifist and he is not made of the type of material that would make a good pacifist. Those who doubt that the great majority of Negroes are not pacifists, just let them slap one. Pick any Negro on any street corner in the U.S.A. and they will find out how much he believes in turning the other cheek.

All those who dare to attack are going to learn the hard way that the Afro-American is not a pacifist, that he cannot forever be counted on not to defend himself. Those who attack him brutally and ruthlessly can no longer expect to attack him with impunity.

The Afro-American cannot forget that his enslavement in this country did not pass because of pacifist moral force or noble appeals to the Christian conscience of the slaveholders.

Henry David Thoreau is idealized as an apostle of nonviolence, the writer who influenced Gandhi, and through

Gandhi, Martin Luther King, Jr. But Thoreau was not dogmatic; his eyes were open and he saw clearly. I keep with me a copy of Thoreau's *Plea For Captain John Brown*. There are truths that are just as evident in 1962 as they were in 1859 when he wrote:

> . . . It was his [John Brown's] peculiar doctrine that a man has a perfect right to interfere by force with the slaveholder, in order to rescue the slave. I agree with him. They who are continually shocked by slavery have some right to be shocked by the violent death of the slaveholder, but such will be more shocked by his life than by his death. I shall not be forward to think him mistaken in his method who quickest succeeds to liberate the slave.
>
> I speak for the slave when I say, that I prefer the philanthropy of Captain Brown to that philanthropy which neither shoots me nor liberates me. . . . I do not wish to kill not to be killed, but I can foresee circumstances in which both these things would be by me unavoidable. We preserve the so-called peace of our community by deeds of petty violence every day. Look at the policeman's billy and handcuffs! Look at the jail! . . . We are hoping only to live safely on the outskirts of this provisional army. So we defend ourselves and our hen-roosts, and maintain slavery. I know that the mass of my countrymen think that the only righteous use that can be made of Sharpe's rifles and revolvers is to fight duels with them, when we are insulted by other nations, or to hunt Indians, or shoot fugitive slaves with them or the like. I think that for once the Sharpe's rifles and the revolvers were employed in a righteous cause. The tools were in the hands of one who could use them.
>
> The same indignation that is said to have cleared the temple once will clear it again. The question is not about the weapon, but the spirit in which you use it. No man has appeared in America, as yet, who loved his fellowman so well, and treated him so tenderly. He [John Brown] lived for him. He took up his life and he laid it down for him. What sort of violence is that which is encouraged, not by soldiers, but by peaceable citizens, not so much by laymen as by ministers of the Gospel, not so much by the fighting sects as by the Quakers, and not so much by Quaker men as by Quaker women?

This event advertises me that there is such a fact as death; the possibility of man's dying. It seems as if no man had ever died in America before; for in order to die you must first have lived.

It is in the nature of the American Negro, the same as all other men, to fight and try to destroy those things that block his path to a greater happiness in life.

"The Future Belongs to Today's Oppressed"

Whenever I speak on the English-language radio station in Havana (which broadcasts for an audience in the United States) I hope in some way to penetrate the mental barriers and introduce new disturbing elements into the consciousness of white America. I hope to make them aware of the monstrous evil that they are party to by oppressing the Negro. Somehow, I must manage to clearly reflect the image of evil that is inherent in a racist society so that white Americans will be able to honestly and fully see themselves as they really are. To see themselves with the same clarity as foreigners see them and to recognize that they are not champions of democracy. To understand that today they do not really even *believe* in democracy. To understand that the world is changing regardless of whether they *think* they like it or not.

For I know that if they had a glimpse of their own reality the shock would be of great therapeutic value. There would be many decent Americans who would then understand that this society must mend its ways if it is to survive, that there is no place in the world now for a racist nation.

As an individual, I'm not inclined toward "politics." The only thing I care about is justice and liberation. I don't belong to any political party. But I think that as long as the present politics prevails the Negro is not going to be integrated into American society. There will have to be great political changes before that can come about.

Those Americans who most deny the logic of the future

Robert and Mabel Williams in September 1996.

are the ones who have driven me into exile. Those people have been cruel. Yet cruel as it may be, this exile was not the end those people had planned for me. But it is not in the hands of today's oppressors to determine my end. Their role in history denies them an understanding of this, just as their role does not allow them to understand that every true nationalist leader in Africa has been imprisoned or exiled and that the future leaders of Latin American and Asian national liberation today are experiencing imprisonment, exile, or worse.

The future belongs to today's oppressed and I shall be witness to that future in the liberation of the Afro-American.

Index

INDEX